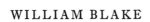

WILLIAM BLAKE

William Blake

H. M. MARGOLIOUTH

ARCHON BOOKS
1967

First published 1961
Oxford University Press

Reprinted 1967 with permission in an
unaltered and unabridged edition

Library of Congress Catalog Card Number: 67-26654
Printed in the United States of America

CONTENTS

ILLUSTRATIONS

All the illustrations are taken from copies in the Print Room
of the British Museum. The first two are from the Macgeorge
copy of *Songs of Innocence and of Experience*, the third from
America, the fourth from *Jerusalem*.

NOTE

QUOTATIONS from Blake have mostly been taken from one or other of the Oxford texts, which have the advantage of line numeration, but for *Milton* and the first two Nights of *The Four Zoas*, where the Nonesuch text has a different arrangement, reference has also been given to that. For Blake's letters I have used the Nonesuch text with the kind consent of Mr. G. L. Keynes.

1950.   H. M. M.

CHAPTER I

THE MAN

ON Sunday 15 October 1752 James Blake and Catherine Harmitage of the parish of St. James's, Westminster (St. James's, Piccadilly) were married at St. George's Chapel, May Fair, as its register shows. This chapel was doing a roaring trade, averaging 1,500 a year, in 'clandestine' marriages. They were, until 1754, perfectly valid in spite of the omission of some formalities, and they were cheap: one guinea covered everything. Of this marriage there were five children who grew up, and no grandchildren. The children were James, William, John, Richard (always called Robert) and Catherine. Of them only William married, and he was childless.

Comparison and contrast with the five members of the Wordsworth family (Richard, William, Dorothy, John and Christopher) suggests itself. Richard Wordsworth succeeded his father as a lawyer and was the rather dull but useful eldest son and business man of the family: James Blake succeeded his father as hosier and haberdasher of 28 Broad Street,[1] Carnaby Market, Golden Square, and, as William Blake's letters and the circumstances of his 1809 Exhibition show, James was of assistance on the business side. In both families the second son was a William and a genius. John Wordsworth was a sailor and died early: John Blake (but 'the evil one') was a soldier and died early. Christopher Wordsworth ('my brother the Dean') was his brother's stand-by in later life: Robert Blake was William's pupil and assistant in early life, his stand-by after his death ('with his spirit I converse daily and

[1] Now 72 Broadwick Street.

hourly in the spirit'). Dorothy and Catherine were only sisters, but otherwise there is contrast: sister Catherine Blake and wife Catherine Blake did not always get on together too well.

Of other relatives not much is known. London trade and Post Office directories (assuming that their entries are correct) show that a hosier's or haberdasher's, or hosier's and haberdasher's, shop was kept at 28 Broad Street by (1) Stephen Blake from at least[1] 1780 to 1784, (2) Blake & Son from at least 1793 to 1806, (3) James Blake from at least 1794 to 1813. In 1814 James Blake, hosier, is at 9 Buckingham Street, Fitzroy Square.[2] It may be inferred (1) that two branches of the Blake family lived in the same house and kept similar shops there, Stephen being a brother or cousin of James Blake the elder (*d.* 1784), and (2) that by 1807 Stephen and Stephen's son had died or otherwise departed, leaving James the younger alone. James moved in 1813 or 1814 to Buckingham Street, but, having bought his annuity, did not go on with the shop for more than a year. There was a cousin (conceivably the aforesaid Stephen) who seems to have lived at one time at Hampstead and to have died well before 1826 when William mentioned him in a letter. There was an aunt who was buried in Bunhill Fields. There were, according to Gilchrist, 'relatives of Blake's father' living at Battersea in 1782.

Into this ordinary London family William Blake was born on 28 November 1757: he was christened at St. James's, Piccadilly, on 11 December. He early showed one of his most marked characteristics—a power of imaginative visualization, whether with the inward or the outward eye. When he was four years old, he was

[1] Omissions mean little, e.g. Parker and Blake (see p. 9) at 27 Broad Street are unmentioned.
[2] Butts (see p. 17) lived in Fitzroy Square.

frightened by seeing God look in through the window. Even if that can be rationalistically explained by the unexpected appearance of some venerable gentleman, the rationalization has little point: it is just the sort of 'vision' young William would have had. A little later he saw a tree at Peckham full of angels—an externalized vision. But it cannot be generically different from what Blake himself wrote in 1810 about the sunrise: 'I see an Innumerable company of the Heavenly host crying: "Holy, Holy, Holy is the Lord God Almighty." I question not my Corporeal or Vegetative Eye any more than I would Question a Window concerning a Sight. I look thro' it & not with it.' Again Tatham, one of the young friends of his old age, records a child-hood vision of Ezekiel. Blake cultivated his visionary power. In his last years he drew 'visionary heads' as from living models. There was no hallucination. He knew that they were not 'as sensible to feeling as to sight'. He also knew that they were not 'the false creation of the heated fancy'. It is the exact opposite of Wordsworth who as a child had sometimes to touch things, to bring in the evidence of a second sense, to make sure they were 'real': such was the power of the gleam of his imagination and so great was the virtue of his 'obstinate questionings of sense and outward things' as an intimation of immortality. Where Wordsworth re-collects his feelings about the daffodils and then sees the daffodils again with the 'inward eye', Blake, so to speak, makes his own daffodils and imposes them on the landscape.

This was the sort of boy who, at the age of ten, instead of going to an ordinary school, went to a drawing-school in the Strand kept by a Mr. Henry Pars. He had begun his professional education. It was still going on when, forty-eight years later, he turned up at the Royal Academy's antique school to make a drawing of the cast of the Laocoön group. This last fact illustrates, as is otherwise evident, that Blake's power of imaginative visualization did not carry with it any exceptional power of memory visualization. The easy way to learn to spell is to see the printed word with the mind's eye: Blake was never a perfectly good or consistent speller. He could not, he found, paint a portrait in the absence of the sitter. Conversely, imaginative painting was hindered by the merely actual. 'If you have not Nature before you for Every Touch', he wrote in a letter in 1802, 'you cannot Paint Portrait; & if you have Nature before you at all, you cannot Paint History.'

Blake was rising fifteen when, on 4 August 1772, he entered on a seven-year apprenticeship, with a fifty guinea premium, to the engraver James Basire of Great Queen Street, Lincoln's Inn Fields. Basire was an engraver of repute in a good way of business. He was fairly old-fashioned. Both he and Pars undoubtedly found in Blake a zealous and hard-working pupil whose interest was not confined to school hours and whose preferences were very decided. His father helped him by buying some casts of classical statuary and enabling him to buy prints which he copied. 'He copied Raphael and Michael Angelo, Martin Hemskerck and Albert Durer, Julio Romano, and the rest of the historic class, neglecting to buy any other prints, however celebrated.'[1] He remained throughout life unshaken in these preferences. His 'Gothic' taste was enhanced, if that were possible, when Basire set him to copy the royal heads and monuments in Westminster Abbey.

Meanwhile the rural ditties were not mute. He wandered, not only by day, over the fields and bathed in the ponds which were easily accessible from his home. He lived then in an ecstatic innocence which he later called 'Jerusalem'.

[1] B. H. Malkin, *A Father's Memoirs of his Child* (1806).

The fields from Islington to Marybone,
To Primrose Hill and Saint John's Wood,
  Were builded over with pillars of gold,
And there Jerusalem's pillars stood.

Her little-ones ran on the fields,
The Lamb of God among them seen,
  And fair Jerusalem his Bride,
Among the little meadows green.

Pancrass & Kentish-town repose
Among her golden pillars high,
  Among her golden arches which
Shine upon the starry sky.

The Jew's-harp-house & the Green Man,
The Ponds where Boys to bathe delight,
  The fields of Cows by Willan's farm,
Shine in Jerusalem's pleasant sight.

Intermittently during these years of apprenticeship he wrote poetry. Some of it was printed, but not published, in 1783 as *Poetical Sketches*. It shows that he read as well as drew. Among his 'favourite studies'[1] were Shakespeare, including *Venus and Adonis*, *Lucrece*, and the *Sonnets*, and Jonson's *Underwoods* and *Miscellanies*. He sets out to imitate Spenser. He must have known Percy's *Reliques*, and he is full of *Ossian*.

The Royal Academy of Arts in London had been founded in 1768. From 1780 and throughout the rest of Blake's life its exhibitions were held in Somerset House. Its schools were already there when, out of his apprenticeship, he continued his studies in them. Moser, the Keeper, tried unsuccessfully to change Blake's taste. Blake, in fact, counter-attacked with a vigour which may well have been thought unbecoming in a pupil. But Blake throughout life was to set principles above persons, his convictions about truth and

[1] Malkin.

reality above all orthodoxies new or old. Of course his
'career' suffered. At present, however, he was in the
coming-young-man class. His friends were other
artists, such as Stothard (born 1755), Flaxman (1755),
Fuseli (1741), Barry (1741). He had no idea of being
merely an engraver of other men's work. He did this,
but he also himself designed, drew, and painted. He
was taken up by 'the accomplished Mrs. Mathew,
whose house, No. 27, in Rathbone Place, was then
frequented by most of the literary and talented people
of the day'.[1] Mr. Mathew is said to have joined
Flaxman in paying for the printing of *Poetical Sketches*
(1783).[2] J. T. Smith, who wrote a short biography of
Blake in 1828, was introduced to the Mathews in 1784
and there he often heard Blake 'read and sing several
of his poems', not necessarily from *Poetical Sketches*.
For—

Much about this time [i.e. of frequenting and then
leaving the Mathew circle], Blake wrote many other
songs, to which he also composed tunes. These he
would occasionally sing to his friends; and though,
according to his confession, he was entirely unac-
quainted with the science of music, his ear was so good,
that his tunes were sometimes most singularly beautiful,
and were noted down by musical professors [i.e. professional musicians].

Here we have the real Blake in his middle twenties.
The 'many other songs' probably included some later
published in *Songs of Innocence*. We notice the first
evidence of an auditory as well as a visual imagination.
In his sixties, in the house of the Linnell family at
Hampstead, he was still singing 'to melodies of his
own'. He died singing. Here too we have the Blake
who described himself in an autograph album in 1826

[1] J. T. Smith.
[2] G. L. Keynes, *Blake Studies* (1949), reckons the cost
at about £6.

as 'one who is very much delighted with being in good Company'. Yet, in spite of the Mathews' kindness, Blake after a while did not feel in good company in their circle, nor did that circle care for his 'unbending deportment' or 'manly firmness of opinion'. Moreover Blake had married. That might keep him more at home, for Mrs. Blake would hardly feel really comfortable with blue-stockings even of the second grade:[1] nor is there any particular reason to suppose that she was invited.

Blake was married on 18 August 1782 at Battersea Church to Catherine Boucher or Butcher, daughter of a market-gardener. He no doubt came to know her through visiting his father's relatives at Battersea. She had fallen in love with him at first sight. The account given by Frederick Tatham, in whose house she spent part of her widowhood, of Blake's appearance at that time may safely be considered hers:

Although not handsome, he must have had a noble countenance, full of expression and animation: his hair was of a yellow brown, and curled with the utmost crispness and luxuriance: his locks, instead of falling down, stood up like a curling flame, and looked at a distance like radiations, which with his fiery eye and expansive forehead, his dignified and cheerful physiognomy, must have made his appearance truly prepossessing.

He was a little man with a large head and wide shoulders. He is almost certainly to be seen, with his Teutonic colouring, in his own picture 'Glad Day' (1780). He was physically very vigorous. The rambles of boyhood were continued in married life. 'In his youth he and his wife would start in the morning early, and walk out twenty miles and dine at some pretty

[1] M. R. Lowery in *Windows of the Morning* shows the improbability of the chief lionesses having frequented the Mathew salon.

and sequestered inn, and would return the same day
home, having travelled forty miles. Mrs. Blake would
do this without excessive fatigue.'[1] He was always
doing something. 'Mrs. Blake has been heard to say
that she never saw him, except when in conversation
or reading, with his hands idle; he scarcely ever mused
upon what he had done.' Even when he was reading,
his hand was often occupied in annotating the book
with his opinions about it. One or other of the tools of
one or other of his arts was generally in his hand. That
explains some of his manuscript remains. This man,
who never sat back with his hands behind his head to
meditate, wrote down those (often unjustifiable)
passing suspicions and bitternesses which most people
feel but do not record.

He suffered in youth, intermittently, from sharp
attacks of abdominal pain which he did not understand
and thought were somehow connected with his rambles
north of London. Later he identified these attacks with
the 'ague' of which he eventually died. This and his
physical vigour, as well as the sense of frustration which
sometimes overcame him, had something to do with
the occasional violence of his temper. He burst out at
Moser, he could throw across the room a plate on which
the engraving would not come out right, he could seize
a dragoon by the elbows and push him helpless a
hundred yards along the road.

This was the man at first sight of whom the gentle
Catherine came so near fainting that she had to leave
'his presence until she had recovered'. Was it a happy
marriage of compatibles? William started by knowing
little of women: Catherine certainly could not really
know William except by living with him. There were
no children: there were some quarrels: there were
occasions, of which the evidence survives, on which
each thought with some bitterness of the other. Yet

[1] Tatham, *Life* (ed. A. G. B. Russell, 1906).

all the evidence, external and internal, combines to show that these were minor and temporary rubs and that the marriage was not merely temperamentally satisfactory but one of true minds. William did not need a stimulus: he needed and found a partner and helpmate. Catherine, in spite of the loss of worldly satisfaction which she may legitimately have expected, felt more than compensated by admission to the world of 'Imagination, the real & eternal World . . . in which we shall live in our Eternal or Imaginative Bodies'. To anyone who merely laughs at such a scale of values Blake is meaningless.

The young couple started in lodgings at 23 Green Street, Leicester Fields (Leicester Square). After two years, in 1784, Blake's father died. His son James took over the hosiery and haberdashery shop at 28 Broad Street, and an astonishing thing happened. Next door, at No. 27, William, too, became a shopkeeper. Together with James Parker, whom he had got to know at Basire's, he set up a print shop and stayed there for three years. He continued to engrave both from his own designs and from those of others and to paint. He published some of his own engravings. There were four of them in the shop—Parker, William, his younger brother Robert to whom he was devoted and who was his pupil, and his wife Catherine. Miss Blake was probably next door helping James and their mother.

In February 1787 an event of utmost importance occurred. Robert died of consumption. The death of John Wordsworth shows in *Peele Castle* and meant much to William Wordsworth. The death of Tom Keats shows in the *Ode to a Nightingale*, and John Keats very likely died as a result of nursing his brother. William Blake nursed his brother without sleep for the last fortnight (was it his intensity of feeling which prevented the other members of the two

B

households taking a turn?) and then slept without a break for three days. He had a vision of Robert's spirit ascending—through the ceiling! (but the provenance of the story is obscure)—clapping hands for joy. In fact, however, William never lost Robert. He remained his *alter ego*. He conversed with him 'daily and hourly in the spirit'. In *Milton* Milton descends to enter into Robert as well as into William. The death of Robert fixed William's attention firmly on 'Eternity'.

After his death Blake and Parker parted company and the Blakes (no longer shopkeeping) moved just round the corner to 28 Poland Street, where they stayed for six years. Here began his association with the Swedenborgians. It was through Flaxman, who had introduced him to the Mathews and was later to introduce him to Hayley, that this came about. Flaxman had joined them before they became, in 1787, a separate sect. Their first chapel was opened in January 1788: in April 1789 a general conference was held which was attended by both Blake and his wife. Both signed the resolutions made at the conference. The members of the New Church continued to meet to discuss Swedenborg's works. Blake was busy this year and the following in reading and annotating them, but he was far too independent to be a mere proselyte. He continued throughout his life to be deeply influenced by some of Swedenborg's doctrines and still more by his method of interpreting the Bible, but Swedenborg's works were still more useful in making Blake think out, or make clear to himself, his own attitude to many fundamental problems. In his own writings he sometimes attacks or deplores Swedenborg and much of *The Marriage of Heaven and Hell* is a satire on Swedenborg, just as Swedenborg's *Heaven and Hell* suggested its title.

Three months after the first Swedenborgian Conference the Bastille fell. Blake was bound to become a revolutionary. He wore the cap of liberty. He consorted with Johnson, the 'left wing' publisher, and Tom Paine. In a flash of insight he gave Paine the advice which sent him to France just in time to avoid arrest. The excitement set him to write poems on both the American and the French revolutions. Yet one may be sceptical about its good effects on Blake as on others. Politics are not good for poets. They kept Milton from his proper work for twenty years. They smothered the poet in Marvell. Wordsworth had to recover from the French Revolution before he could do his best work. The twist it gave to Blake has been held, not implausibly, to be partly responsible for his later obscurity. It is, indeed, a poet's business to be imaginatively aware of the grandeur and the pathos of the actions of men individually and in the mass and to penetrate intuitively to the springs of those actions: he may lament over the Jerusalem that has fallen or exult at the Jerusalem that is to be built in a kingdom not of this world: but, in so far as he sets out to promote the concrete aims of any political faction, he cannot be a poet, whatever else he may be. Shelley on kings and priests is childish. He could be a great poet in the spirit of the French Revolution only because its body was dead. Blake, we shall find, failed as a mere rebel, but was magnificent in his constructive imagination.

The third event of this year 1789 was the 'publication' of *Songs of Innocence*. Its importance lies not only in its contents, but in its method of publication—the only method by which any of his books (if we except descriptive matter connected with the exhibition of his pictures in 1809) was ever published in his lifetime. Blake was his own publisher. There was no typesetting or printing from type. Each page of the book-to-be was engraved like a picture on a copper plate, and impressions were taken off in the ordinary way. But there was this difference. The usual method is to cut the lines and shades of the picture with a hard graving-tool on the comparatively soft copper, then to ink the plate but remove the ink from the flat surfaces leaving it only in the engraved lines, then to apply paper and so print from it. Blake adopted an opposite method. First he wrote his words and drew his pictures on the plate in some liquid impervious to acid, then he applied acid to eat away the surface of the rest of the plate leaving the words and pictures in relief, then he applied ink or colour-wash and so printed, the pictorial part being finished off by hand with watercolour. This is Blake's celebrated Illuminated Printing. It was perhaps first suggested to him by the illuminated manuscripts of the middle ages. To this combination of relief and colour printing he was directed in a vision by his dead brother, Robert. He used it first for a little 'tractate', *There is No Natural Religion*, but *Songs of Innocence*, which contained 31 plates or pages (17 leaves), was the first real book published in this way. It will be realized that, with this method of printing and publication, copies will be few and each copy may differ from all the others. There may be changes in the colours used, changes may be made in the plates, or something may be added to or painted out on a particular print.

Why did Blake produce and publish his books in this unusual way? There is only one real answer: he wanted to produce the sort of book which could only be produced in this way. To turn the pages of one of the twenty odd copies of *Songs of Innocence* which survive is still to have a rare experience. The meaning and the music of the words, the designs decorative, symbolic or illustrative, the richness and variety of the colouring, all flow together to produce beauty of dream-like uniqueness and immeasurable depth. That was the soul of Blake in the year of the French Revolution. Not even Keats's Grecian Urn 'in midst of other woe' remains more 'a friend to man'.

He wanted to produce just this combination of poetry and painting, and that may well be the reason why he had not cared, six years previously, to publish the printed copies of *Poetical Sketches* in their mere naked black on white. Flaxman (and perhaps Mr. Mathew) had paid for that printing. It may be true that he could not afford, i.e. did not want to spend his money on, ordinary printing. It is certainly true that Blake was a keen experimenter, very skilful and knowledgeable in the technique of his craft, not in the least content to amble on beaten tracks. This was only the first of his inventions in colour-printing. Not all the details of his method or the media he used are known for certain. It is interesting to remember Blake as a technical inventor. One reason for the relief etching may have been that, since the words had to be written backwards on the copper plate to come out right on the print, it was much easier to write them with a pen in the impervious liquid than to cut them with a graving-tool.[1]

During the rest of his time in Poland Street Blake thought more about political and social questions than ever before or after. There or immediately after moving from there he wrote *Songs of Experience* in which we find war, prostitution, poverty, punishment. He wrote the first book of a poem on *The French Revolution* and its companion, *America, A Prophecy*. He wrote in *Visions of the Daughters of Albion* of the miseries of enforced chastity and enforced marriage. He became also more deeply concerned with other, fundamental, questions. *The Book of Thel* shows a soul only just saved from utter despair at its own apparent uselessness. *The Marriage of Heaven and Hell* attempts to outmode current conceptions of good and evil. He made an engraving of Job, a

[1] Blake may have varied his method: see Keynes, *William Blake's Engravings*, (1950), p. 19.

subject which was to be with him to the end of his life.

All these works and some others are included in a remarkable etched Prospectus, dated October 10, 1793, which Blake issued several months after leaving Poland Street for 13 Hercules Buildings, Lambeth. (His mother had died in the previous year, but it is not known why he moved across the river). It shows Blake's confidence in himself as 'the Man of Genius' (later he called himself 'a Mental Prince') and in the method he had invented 'of Printing both Letter-press and Engraving in a style more ornamental, uniform, and grand, than any before discovered, while it produces works at less than one fourth of the expense'. 'The Illuminated Books are Printed in Colours, and on the most beautiful wove paper that could be procured.'

In Lambeth the Blakes remained until their removal in September 1800 to Felpham. To Lambeth belong the stories of the vine that Blake would not prune, of William and Catherine caught acting Adam and Eve in the summer-house, of their being so well-off that they were burgled of quite a substantial amount, of generosity to the deserving and the undeserving, of Blake's interference on behalf of the boy who was badly treated at Astley's circus. In the earlier part of this period came out what are often called the Lambeth books, *America*, *Europe*, and the Books of *Urizen*, *Ahania* and *Los* and *The Song of Los*. We are confronted by the problem of the strange names Blake invented.

He invented them for the same sort of reason as led him to invent his illuminated printing: he wanted to do something which could not be done by any existing means. He wanted to describe the workings of mind in the past, present, and future. The current abstract terms, such as Reason, Nature, the Ruling Passion, simply would not do. They were too vague, they did not go deep enough, and they were abstract. Blake

knew that it is not abstractions which move the world.
The eighteenth century with its passion for personification was groping after something genuine. The terms
of classical mythology would have been nearer the
mark, but they would not have been correct terms,
they were too hackneyed, and they were not supposed
to be real in the sense that Blake needed. He needed a
set of new technical terms which were not abstractions
but described something real, alive, and active. The
same thing has been done afresh in the present century by the psychologists. Id, Ego, Censor, Anima,
Shadow are conceptions not far removed from Blake's:
in fact some of his terms have been almost equated
with some of Jung's. But no facile substitution of
another set of names for Blake's will do. The only
way to understand just what Blake meant by Urizen
or Los is to study what Urizen or Los does or suffers
in Blake's poems and pictures: moreover they develop,
just as Mr. Pickwick developed from a comic local
antiquary into the genial friend and counsellor.

About the origin of the names themselves there has
been much guesswork. One of the few certain things
is that the form of some of the names, especially
terminations in -on or -mon, is due to *Ossian*. In fact
the whole conception of such a terminology could have
been suggested by *Ossian*, which Blake could very well
have read in a Blakean sense as an account of mental
happenings. Blake's Theotormon, Bromion, and
Oothoon have a connection with the names of Macpherson's Tonthormod, Brumo, and Oithona. Blake's
Leutha was once Macpherson's Lutha. But his reading
was wide. Urizen, who is in some respects a sort of
Jupiter, may have been formed from a passage in
Bryant's *Ancient Mythology*, where Ουριον Ζηνα
(*Ourion Zena* translated 'Great Urian Jove') occurs.
Rintrah may come from Indra. Orc is from the latin
Orcus (Hell). Los, who, though always a smith, is a

mental smith, *may* be a partial anagram of 'soul'. Enitharmon, the chief female personage in the books of the Lambeth period, is Ossianic in termination, but her two first syllables look like an imperfect reversal of the last two syllables of Catherine. To many of the names there is not even the beginning of a clue. It is perhaps as well, for it is not the origin of a name but what Blake comes to mean by it that is important, and the whole system of names emphasizes Blake's individuality and originality. 'I must Create a System or be enslav'd by another Man's', he wrote in *Jerusalem*: but, of course, no one was less a system-creator than Blake nor less likely to be enslaved by another man's.

In the later 'Lambeth books' Blake set out to give his version of how paradise was lost. As in Milton, a fall of the Angels leads to the Creation of the finite world; the primal sin is not exactly pride but separateness, self-sufficingness. We all know at times the horror of the limited, isolated self. That isolation, self-sought, is the original evil in *The Book of Urizen*. This set of books, however, rather peters out. Not only is there no hint of how paradise may be regained, but Blake must have felt that there was something inadequate about them as a mental history of the world. He began again in 1797. His new work was in nine 'Nights' on the analogy of Young's *Night Thoughts*, for an edition of which he had been occupied on the vastest of his book-illustration engagements. In this work jealousy (a word which will often be better understood in Blake if we substitute the modern 'possessiveness') is the root of mental evil, and the worst jealousy is that of the mental faculties or elements against one another— Reason, Instinct, Emotion and Imagination. On this work *Vala* or *The Four Zoas*, which he never published, Blake was still engaged in 1800 when he moved from Lambeth to Felpham on the Sussex coast.

The Lambeth years were the most prosperous of

Blake's life. They saw his second important technical invention, that of the colour-printing of pictures from millboard (pasteboard, i.e. board made of several thicknesses of paper stuck together), and many of his finest pictures. He also had many pupils, who are said to have found him a most interesting talker.[1] A suggestion that he might be engaged to teach drawing in the royal family[1] appalled him: he saw himself on the edge of an abyss of worldliness and mere moneymaking in which what he was meant to be and do would be lost. He gave up most of his teaching to concentrate on what mattered. The father of one of his pupils was the Muster-Master-General, Thomas Butts: he gave Blake a commission for fifty pictures. Flaxman introduced him to William Hayley, a poet and a man of means, who was writing his *Life of Cowper*. Hayley invited Blake to engrave illustrations for it and to settle at Felpham. Blake's friends, who had begun to be disturbed at the possible effects of his quixotry on his means of livelihood and urged him to moderate his unorthodoxies, thought it a great chance. So did the Blakes in their different way. The hackneyed modern use of 'thrilled' best expresses their feelings both before and after the journey to Felpham. It was a delightful journey with six changes of chaise for the Blakes and their 'Sixteen heavy boxes & portfolios full of prints. And Now Begins a New life.'

Felpham was a failure. It was a continuous crisis of three years' duration resolved by the sacrificial decision to return to London. We have a great deal of information about this period. Of 89 surviving letters by Blake 46 belong to the five years 1800–1804 and 15 of them, including most of the longest and most important, were written from Felpham. Butts was the recipient of most of those written from Felpham: those written to Felpham, after and before Blake's

[1] Tatham.

stay there, were to Hayley. After the initial delight of arriving at a beautiful place in a fine September and being welcomed with 'brotherly affection' there were a few months when all seemed to go well. Blake settled down to the 'heads of the poets' and to commissions for miniatures: he had promised to be 'the determined advocate of Religion & Humility, the two bands of Society'. Hayley, as patron, was busy setting and finding him work, even to the decoration of ladies' fans: he read aloud to him Klopstock in translation: he took him out riding, but Hayley carried an umbrella on horseback and was always falling off. This well-meaning, slightly ridiculous man of talent, who thought himself Virgil and Maecenas in one, could not permanently harness Blake, a most individual genius. Blake realized his kindliness. He kept his temper under control or only let it out to write an epigram in a private notebook. But the question of going back began to agitate him before November 1801, and at last Blake could hold himself in no longer. There was some sort of a scene[1], after which friendly relations were resumed with a difference; Blake could not stay. Hayley, a 'corporeal friend', was a 'spiritual enemy', but to give up the corporeal friend might mean starvation. Blake knew he was meant to do 'Spiritual Acts'. He heard a voice within which said, 'If you, who are organized by Divine Providence for spiritual communion, Refuse, & bury your Talent in the Earth, even tho' you should want Natural Bread, Sorrow & Desperation pursues you thro' life, & after death shame & confusion of face to eternity. . . . You will be called the base Judas who betray'd his Friend !'

Domestic troubles were added. The 'beautiful' cottage with its 'thatched roof of rusted gold' gave Mrs. Blake 'Agues & Rheumatism'. Blake's sister was living with them and the two Kates did not get on well

[1] See Frye, *Fearful Symmetry*, p. 329.

together. There was a plan early in 1803 to move to a 'village further from the Sea, Perhaps Lavant'. In the spring it was decided, 'with the full approbation of Mr. Hayley', to return to London in September when the three years for which the cottage had been taken would be up.

A month before the Blakes were due to leave the cottage, on 12 August 1803, happened one of those totally unexpected things which have the most alarming immediate consequences and which leave a permanent mark. Blake told a dragoon named Scholfield to go out of his garden. He would not go, but 'threaten'd to knock out my Eyes, with many abominable imprecations & with some contempt for my Person'. Blake flared up, took him by the elbows and pushed him out. At the gate the dragoon turned round to fight. Blake, that contemptible little man, dashed out, seized him again by the elbows and ran him up the road to the Fox Inn, where he was billeted. Four days later Blake appeared before the Bench at Chichester to answer Scholfield's sworn information that, in the course of the fracas, he had made treasonable exclamations against king and country. The war with France had been resumed in the previous May and an invasion threat to the south coast was in men's minds. Blake might be a spy. We remember Wordsworth and Coleridge at Alfoxden in 1797, after the French ships had come up the Bristol Channel and then landed 1,500 men on the Pembrokeshire coast: Coleridge made fun of the way the detective set to watch them might hear them talking about Spinoza and report their intimacy with 'Spy nosy'. Scholfield really did something like that. He reported that Blake was a military painter, having heard of his miniatures. This, however, did not come into the indictment, which included a charge of assault on Scholfield. The matter lasted five months. Blake was allowed bail. He appeared at General Quarter Sessions at Petworth on 4 October, and again at General Quarter Sessions at Chichester on 10 January. Evidence was submitted both for the Crown and for Blake. His counsel, William Rose, was able to produce Scholfield's previous bad record and to convince the jury of the likelihood of his perjury. Blake was acquitted.

Hayley acted splendidly. He was one of the two besides Blake himself who went bail for him. He provided counsel and bestirred himself in every possible way. Blake was aware of it and regretted that he had previously unburdened himself to Butts: 'burn what I have peevishly written about any friend'. He returned to London as arranged and in October thanked Hayley for 'your generous & tender solicitude about your devoted rebel'. But the return had in any case been a risk. These months of anxiety (death or transportation was quite probable) and journeyings to Sussex to stand trial were the worst possible start. Mrs. Blake had been, and probably remained, terrified, but the danger clinched their mutual devotion and determination to keep 'the Divine Vision in time of trouble'.

Blake did not feel that the Felpham years had been wasted. He had cleared up his views about art. He had completed, revised more than once, and abandoned *The Four Zoas*. A good deal of it was to be incorporated in *Milton* and *Jerusalem*, written in the rooms at 17 South Molton Street which he was to occupy for eighteen years. After that he was to spend six final years in rooms at 3 Fountain Court, off the south side of the Strand, where one of Mrs. Blake's sisters and her husband, Mr. Banes or Baines, lived.

The twenty-four years between Blake's return from Felpham and his death fall into three roughly equal periods. First there are the years of renewed inspiration and effort, punctuated by bitter events, and ending in obvious worldly failure. Then came a time of obscurity and poverty in the course of which *Jerusalem* was finished but its author had even to make drawings of soup tureens and other table-ware to get a bare subsistence. Finally a group of younger artists became Blake's friends and helpers and, to some extent, disciples. His sixties were mostly years of mellow happiness and achievement, of the Job and Dante series. From some of these young men, notably Linnell and Tatham, we know much of him in his last years, and also from Crabb Robinson, that Boswell to all men. Blake was not lacking in 'good company' at the last.

In 1803 he had made the great decision. In September of that year he gave up all certain prospects to keep 'the Divine Vision'. In that same month William and Dorothy Wordsworth returned from their great and fruitful tour in the Highlands to find Mary snugly at home with the child born in the previous June. From that time on Wordsworth by slow but steady stages made a decision the reverse of Blake's. The *Ode to Duty* is the saddest and most lingering of farewells to that for which Wordsworth was specially 'organized by Divine Providence'. Prudence, or what Blake calls 'Moral Virtue', won. If Blake had had a family to provide for and Wordsworth had not, would both decisions have been different?

At first things did not seem too bad. Mrs. Blake, having been brought 'near the gate of death' by rheumatism and anxiety, had by the end of 1804 recovered after a long course of electrical treatment. Blake was still corresponding with Hayley and doing illustrations for him. Butts was a steady patron. But it was difficult, after his three years' absence from London, for Blake to get back his engraving connexion. There was plenty of work but other engravers got it. The very fact that he badly needed it militated, of course, against his getting it. When he was employed, it led to a series of unpleasantnesses. First, one Cromek decided to bring out an illustrated edition of Blair's *The Grave* (1743), one of those meditations on death of which the eighteenth century, in its different way, was quite as fond as the seventeenth. He commissioned Blake, verbally, to design the illustrations, which Blake, for a considerably larger payment, was subsequently to engrave. He gave the engraving work to another man, named Schiavonetti. The evidence that he cheated Blake is conclusive. There also survives a letter from Cromek to Blake in which he jeers at Blake and his poverty; he was a very nasty and unscrupulous character. The second trouble was also due to Cromek, though the details are less clear. Before the breach with Blake he found Blake beginning work on a picture of Chaucer's Canterbury Pilgrims. He went to Stothard and suggested this subject to him. Stothard set to work and produced his picture, which was exhibited with great success while Blake's was not yet finished. Cromek's villainy is certain, but it is not certain that Stothard was aware that once again (in Fuseli's words) Blake was 'damned good to steal from'. Blake naturally supposed he was aware, and he was embittered against his old friend.

Blair's *Grave* came out in 1808. Blake was at once attacked by Robert Hunt, brother of Leigh Hunt, in the *Examiner*. He found Blake's allegory, in which the soul is symbolized by a bodily form, absurd. He found Blake's nudes 'libidinous'. This article was the third of Blake's troubles. The fourth was the failure of an exhibition which he held in 1809, a failure no doubt due, in part at least, to a second attack in the *Examiner*. 'The praises . . . bestowed last year on this unfortunate man's illustrations of *Blair's Grave*, have, in feeding his vanity, stimulated him to publish his madness more largely, and thus again exposed him, if not to the derision, at least to the pity of the public.' The exhibition failed, but it and a projected successor were the occasion of Blake's most sustained prose writing. The published *Descriptive Catalogue*, the unpublished *Public Address* and *Vision of the Last Judgment*[1] and the letters provide an essential help to understanding Blake.

By 1811 worldly failure in respect of both fame and fortune was complete. In no year does he actually disappear from view. Southey visited him in 1811. In 1812 he exhibited three pictures at the exhibition of the Associated Artists in Water Colour. We have a relief-etching dated 1813. In 1814 he began engraving plates for Flaxman's *Hesiod*. In 1815 he had a bread-and-butter commission from Wedgwood of Etruria to draw and engrave specimens of his table-ware for his private catalogues. 'Terrines', creambowls, butter-boats were sent in small numbers to him to copy at home. The only letter from Blake extant between 1809 and 1818 is to Wedgwood. Perhaps it was partly urgent need for a change from crockery that made him in 1815 go to the Royal Academy's antique school to copy the Laocoön. In 1816 he was still engraving for Wedgwood, and in that year T. F. Dibdin, a friend of Isaac D'Israeli (himself a purchaser of some of Blake's work), records a visit from and a conversation with him. He was also at work in that year on designs for *L'Allegro* and *Il Penseroso*. A watercolour ('The Judgment of Paris') is dated 1817, the year in which the *Hesiod* engravings were published. During these years *Jerusalem* was being finished, and in or about 1818 the octosyllabic paragraphs of *The Everlasting Gospel* were written down in odd spaces of a notebook which had once been Robert's and which Blake had been using for drawings and writings at intervals since Robert died.

[1] Headed *Advertizement* and *Catalogue for the year 1810* in Sloss and Wallis, *William Blake's Prophetic Writings*, vol. II.

In 1818 the last, mellow phase began. We know a great deal about Blake's outward appearance during it. Although the portrait by Thomas Phillips in the National Portrait Gallery belongs to 1807 (an engraving from it was prefixed in 1808 to Blair's *Grave*), T. F. Dibdin reports no change in 1816—'his stature mean, his head big and round, his forehead broad and high, his eyes blue, large and lambent—such as my friend Mr. Phillips has represented him upon his imperishable canvas'. In 1820 John Linnell made a pencil drawing of head and shoulders. Below the massive forehead and bald front of the head (he is not bald in Phillips's portrait) Blake looks downward, apparently with partially closed eyes. He may be at work with brush or graver. He looks old. In September 1821 Linnell drew Blake and Varley disputing in Linnell's house in Cirencester Place. The face (right profile) is that of the 1827 miniature without the wrinkles. Both sit at a table, Varley gesticulating eagerly, Blake with right elbow drawn tautly back and suggesting concentration. About 1825 Linnell drew him in the open air at Hampstead: three-quarter face and with a hat on he looks much younger, rather like a fifty year old farmer. Blake's own 'visionary portrait' of himself belongs to this last decade. It is obviously something of a joke and we note that he has got his hair back, though it hangs down in unfamiliar straight locks. The life mask made by a phrenologist named Deville in 1823 greatly exaggerates the habitual compression of the lips: the closed eyes and flattened hair combine with that to make it a much less trustworthy indication of Blake's usual appearance than Linnell's three sketches. And no wonder: having a life mask made is not a pleasant experience and on this occasion 'the plaster pulled out a quantity of his hair'. Consequently 'that is not like dear Blake's mouth, such a look of severity was foreign to him—an expression of sweetness and sensibility being habitual'. So reports George Richmond, the youngest of the young friends of Blake's age. He also sketched[1] Blake in pencil—full length, out walking. It must be admitted that the drawing made by Tatham of Blake aged 69, in which both the compression of the lips and the down-turning of the snub nose are marked, recalls the life mask. The year 1826, however, had been one of physical pain of more than one sort. More wrinkled but less grim is Linnell's 1827 miniature on ivory.

Of Blake's new set of young friends the first was John Linnell (1792–1882), who was introduced to him in 1818 by another young man, George Cumberland, son of one of Blake's early friends. These young men were all artists. Their birth and death dates should both be noticed. They were young when they knew Blake, and many of them were alive when Gilchrist's *Life* (published 1863) was being written and were available for supplying information. These young men provided Blake at last with a whole group to appreciate him and his work. Without their encouragement there might have been no 'Job' or 'Dante'. Linnell was a portrait and landscape painter. The group included Samuel Palmer (1805–1881), landscape-painter and watercolourist, who first met Blake in 1824, having exhibited at the Royal Academy at the age of fourteen; Edward Calvert (1799–1883), an idyllic painter who had been in the Navy but settled in London in 1824; Francis Oliver Finch (1802–62), landscape painter and watercolourist, a pupil of John Varley (1778–1842), whom Linnell introduced to Blake in 1819 and who stimulated Blake to draw the 'visionary heads'; Henry Walter (1790–1849), painter of animals in landscape; George Richmond (1809–96), portrait-painter, who was only sixteen when first brought to meet Blake;

[1] Reproduced as frontispiece to K. Preston, *Blake and Rossetti* (1944).

and Frederick Tatham (1805–78), sculptor, Blake's executor.

The young men called the house where Blake lived 'The House of the Interpreter'. From 1821 he had two rooms on the first floor of the not undignified eighteenth-century house in Fountain Court. He remained poor: in the year in which he removed there he had to sell the collection of prints which he had started to form when a boy at Pars's school in the Strand nearby. One of the two rooms was his show and sale room: it was hung with his work, of some of which he from time to time made fresh copies. In the other, the back room but with a side-window looking on the Thames and the Surrey hills, Blake and his wife cooked, ate, worked, received visitors, and slept. Sometimes sleep was interrupted by inspiration. William would get up and set to work, and his wife got up too and sat beside him. It helped. They were completely at one. After his death he came and sat by her, daily, sometimes for two or three hours.

Except for *The Ghost of Abel*, engraved on two plates in 1822, no new poetry was written during these last years. Blake had turned from 'prophetic' poems with pictorial comment to 'prophetic' pictures with written comment. Instead of an engraved plate of poetry with a festoon of human figures we have a 'Job' engraving surrounded by text. In the 'Laocoön', probably engraved about 1820, the change is most strikingly shown: even some of the spaces between the human and serpentine figures are occupied by words, just as in earlier days Blake would fill in any spare space on the page of poetry with some little drawing.

Linnell was a patron as well as a friend and disciple (Hayley had been patron and friend but he wanted to be tutor, not disciple). Nineteen letters, mostly short, from Blake to him and two to Mrs. Linnell survive in addition to documents recording their business dealings. Blake paid visits to him at Hampstead, but attacks of his illness begin to be mentioned in 1824, and in July 1826 'our intended flight into your delightful country' has to be put off because of sudden cold weather. The wasting disease of which he was to die next year does not seem to have been understood at all; it brought on 'a species of delirium' and 'Pain too much for Thought'. The pain was intermittent, but, in spite of 'getting better every morning', he got weaker and weaker—'feeble and tottering, but not in spirit and life, not in the real man, the imagination, which liveth for ever. In that I am stronger and stronger, as this foolish body decays.' It was true: the unfinished but magnificent 'Dante' series was done at this time, much of it in bed. In bed he did for Tatham the colour-print of 'The Ancient of Days', now in the Whitworth Institute, Manchester. His death is famous. He made his arrangements: he would be buried where his relations lay, in Bunhill Fields, and with the Church of England service. He saw heaven and sang of it, and so died in the early evening of Sunday, 12 August 1827.

His wife survived four years, spent partly in rooms of her own, partly in Linnell's London house and partly as Tatham's housekeeper. James Blake, the last of the brothers, had died in 1824. The sister, Catherine, lived long after Mrs. Blake. The date of her death is unknown. She is said to have become very poor.

CHAPTER II

THE PICTORIAL ARTIST

IT cannot be too strongly emphasized that Blake was primarily an artist in the narrower sense of that word. The only schools he ever attended were art schools. He never published a book of poems in which words were not linked with design and of which the methods of production and sale were not those of the artist rather than the poet. His poems thus form no exception to the rule that he made his living by engraving and painting. He did a great deal of engraving of other men's designs. The revised (1945) *Everyman* edition of Gilchrist's *Life* includes a list of fifty-five books containing illustrations engraved by Blake but not designed by him. The list includes poets from Chaucer onwards, novels, geography books, art books, history books. In some of them only one or two of the engravings are by Blake, e.g. a complete Josephus (about 1786) has out of sixty illustrations three only engraved by Blake and *A New System of Geography* (1785) has one only. Sometimes, where there is no corroborative evidence, it is possible that the engraver was not our Blake but another. Nevertheless the list is important as an indication both of Blake's mere bread-and-butter work and of the wide range of books of which that work brought him cognizance.

Besides book illustrations Blake did other engraving of other men's pictures, such as Cosway's 'Venus and Adonis', but our principal interest, of course, is in his original work. That may be considered under the two main headings of (1) engravings and drawings made with a view to engraving and (2) paintings.

Blake's engraved books, ranging in bulk from the two

plates of *The Ghost of Abel* to the hundred of *Jerusalem*, number seventeen. Of these one, *The Gates of Paradise*, consisted in its first form (1793) of pictures and titles only. The other sixteen are, in approximate chronological order, *There is No Natural Religion, Songs of Innocence, All Religions are One, The Book of Thel, The Marriage of Heaven and Hell, America, Visions of the Daughters of Albion, Songs of Experience, Europe, The Book of Urizen, The Song of Los, The Book of Ahania, The Book of Los, Milton, Jerusalem* and *The Ghost of Abel.* These seventeen books stretch over the years from 1788 to 1822, but Blake's engravings began in his apprentice days. Unsigned engravings in Gough's *Sepulchral Monuments in Great Britain* were probably done by Blake for Basire, and the first form of 'Joseph of Arimathea among the Rocks of Albion' dates from 1773, when Blake was only sixteen.

His principal book illustrations are a series of six for Mary Wollstonecraft's *Original Stories from Real Life* (1791 edition), of forty-three for Young's *Night Thoughts* (1797—the number of drawings, all extant, which Blake did was 537), of seventeen for Hayley's *Ballads* (1802 and 1805), of twenty-two (including the title page) 'Illustrations of the Book of Job' (1825): to these must be added Blake's only wood-engravings, the seventeen (exclusive of three engraved by another hand) designs to Thornton's *Pastorals of Virgil.* Further there are the Blair's *Grave* series (1808) designed but not engraved by Blake, the twenty-eight watercolour drawings illustrating *The Pilgrim's Progress* (made in 1824 but not engraved or published), and the hundred and two drawings illustrating Dante, of which seven were engraved at the end of Blake's life.

The greatest of the single engravings not included above represent 'Job's Complaint' (1793), 'The Death of Ezekiel's Wife' (1793), 'Chaucer's Canterbury Pilgrims' (1810—an engraving of Blake's 'fresco' painting) and Milton's 'Mirth and Her Companions' (*L'Allegro*), which probably belongs to 1818 or thereabouts.

Though the division is convenient, there is really no hard and fast line to be drawn between the drawings and engravings on the one hand and the paintings on the other. The two sets of watercolour designs which preceded the 'Job' engravings might come under either head: so might the *Pilgrim's Progress* and 'Dante' series. The colour-prints will come under painting and yet are not exactly paintings in the ordinary sense of the word. The relief-engravings or etchings were all meant to be coloured. W. M. Rossetti, who made the first list of Blake's pictures for Gilchrist's *Life*, excluded the relief-engravings from his list of 'works in colour', but included the drawings for 'Job', *Pilgrim's Progress*, and 'Dante'. He has 262 items, but counts a series as one. If each picture in a series were counted separately, the number of coloured works would come to nearly twice that. Blake was fondest of watercolour or distemper, but he had used oil too. It is important to remember that he thought much about and experimented much with the technique and materials of his art. When he talks of despair or illumination, it is always possible that it is not about God or Man but some problem of technical process. By early training and personal predilection he believed strongly in clear outline. It can be seen in everything he drew. So he is for Michelangelo and draughtsmanship and against Titian and the colourists. Chiaroscuro was anathema to him. 'The more distinct, sharp, and wirey the bounding line, the more perfect the work of art.'

The paintings include several Miltonic series— *Paradise Lost*, *Paradise Regained*, the Hymn *On the Morning of Christ's Nativity*, *Comus*, *L'Allegro*, and *Il Penseroso* all supplied the subject-matter for a set of paintings. So, though unknown to Rossetti, did Gray's poems. Indeed the subjects of most of Blake's paintings were literary, if under that we include biblical and historical: the Bible, in fact, is an easy first. Inspiration and treatment are always Blake's own. There is no question of merely antiquarian or representational verisimilitude. The painter of 'The Spiritual Form of Nelson guiding Leviathan' was not likely to be troubled about a Babylonian background for his 'Nebuchadnezzar': yet he could, because he wished, combine visual accuracy with symbolism in 'Sir Jeffery Chaucer and the Nine-and-twenty Pilgrims on their journey to Canterbury'. In general he made a sharp distinction: 'Historical Designing is one thing & Portrait Painting another, & they are as Distinct as any two Arts can be. Happy would that Man be who could unite them!'

Blake did not try to unite them. Though he believed strongly in the educative value of exact copying, he disliked drawing from a model and found 'Nature' a hindrance. 'In my Brain are studies & Chambers filled with books & pictures of old, which I wrote & painted in ages of Eternity before my mortal life': to reproduce for our limited senses and with our limited materials these works stored in his imagination ('the real man') was his aim. He made no attempt

> from outward forms to win
> The passion and the life, whose fountains are within.

He was a great colourist of the Florentine, not the Venetian kind. What effect a visit to Italy might have had on his theory and practice has been the subject of vain speculations. We have what we have: at its best it is unique and superb. Some of his work is unfinished, the colouring of some has not proved permanent, but the best examples of the colour-prints and of the illuminated books are incomparable in their richness and delicacy. Colour may have been less important in Blake's conscious mind than line and composition, but it opens a window on his imagination which is not to be neglected. Unfortunately, the systematic examination, cataloguing and reproducing of the whole of Blake's pictorial work has still to be done. W. M. Rossetti's catalogue (1863) is still the only attempt at a complete one.[1] A few good colour reproductions have been made, but, though no reproduction on smooth paper can ever be the same as the original with the actual paint, the mere literary student of Blake needs urgently to be provided both with a definitive catalogue raisonné and with a complete set of coloured reproductions of, at least, the best examples of each of Blake's pictorial and illuminated works. He has been too much condemned to read Blake's poetry in a form never seen by Blake himself (except for the unpublished *Poetical Sketches* and the unpublished *French Revolution*)—the ordinary printed page.

D. G. Rossetti, writing in his Supplementary chapter to Gilchrist's *Life* (1863), suggested that Blake as a colourist was the fore-runner of the Pre-Raphaelite Brotherhood. At any rate his exposition of Blake as a colourist would be hard to beat.

His most original and prismatic system of colour, in which tints laid on side by side, each in its utmost force, are made by masterly treatment to produce a startling and novel effect of truth. . . . In Blake's colouring of landscape a subtle and exquisite reality forms quite as strong an element as does ideal grandeur; whether we find him dealing with the pastoral sweetness of drinking cattle at a stream, their hides and fleeces all glorified by sunset with magic rainbow hues, or revealing to us, in a flash of creative genius, some parted sky and beaten sea full of portentous expectation. One unfailing

[1] There is Wright's (*Life*, II. pp. 128–182), but that is an index rather than an ordered catalogue.

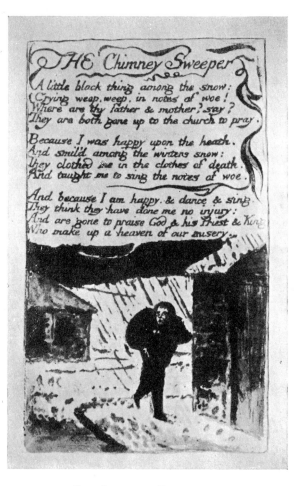

From SONGS OF EXPERIENCE

Same size as original design

sign of his true brotherhood with all the great colourists is the lovingly wrought and realistic flesh-painting which is constantly to be met with in the midst of his most extraordinary effects. For pure realism, too, though secured in a few touches as only greatness can, let us turn to the dingy London street, all snow-clad and smoke-spotted, through which the little black chimney-sweeper wends his way in the *Songs of Experience*. Certainly an unaccountable perversity in colour may now and then be apparent, as where, in the same series, the tiger is painted in fantastic streaks of red, green, blue, and yellow, while a tree stem at his side tantalisingly supplies the tint which one might venture to think his due and is perfect tiger-colour! I am sure, however, that such vagaries, curious enough no doubt, are not common with Blake, as the above is the only striking instance I can recall in his published work. But, perhaps, a few occasional bewilderments may be allowed to a system of colour which is often suddenly called upon to help in embodying such conceptions as painter never before dreamed of: some old skeleton folded together in the dark bowels of earth or some symbolic human birth of crowned flowers at dawn, amid rosy light and the joyful opening of all things. Even a presentment of the most abstract truths of natural science is not only attempted by this new painter, but actually effected by legitimate pictorial ways and we are somehow shown, in figurative yet not wholly unreal shapes and hues, the mingling of organic substances, the gradual development and perpetual transfusion of life.

Blake as a colourist must be studied at first hand in libraries and picture-galleries, at second hand in reproductions (of which the number is at present quite inadequate) in expensive books, but also in the postcard reproductions issued by, for example, the Tate Gallery.

If Blake's colouring gives us an insight into his mind which the literary student dares not neglect, so does his composition. The elements of it are the horizontal line, the vertical line and the curve. That is platitude, but Blake's use of these elements and their counterpoint is often very striking. The hundred plates of Figgis's *The Paintings of William Blake* (1925) may be used in exemplification. Plate 1, 'The Ancient of Days' (originally the frontispiece to *Europe*, 1794, but the last copy was made for Tatham by Blake on his death-bed in 1827), shows a creator inside a circle (the sun symbolizing Time). His immense left shin and left arm form the central vertical lines ending in a pair of shining compasses which diverge to left and right (the meaning of left arm and foot will appear later when we arrive at 'Job', but it should be noted that, at least in the 1827 copy, there is beside the left foot a paw-like duplicate[1] of it which has unspiritual suggestions). The horizontal lines are provided mainly by the creator's long white hair and beard which some great wind from his left is blowing to the right at a right angle to the downstretched left arm. What wind is that? Or had even Blake sometimes to ask questions rather than give answers?

Plate 2, 'The Angel of the Divine Presence Clothing Adam and Eve with Coats of Skins', is a watercolour dated 1803. It is astonishing to think of the painter of this even attempting to keep step with Hayley and his like. The curve is provided by overarching vegetation (i.e. the world of matter and the senses) which frames a background of sky against which stands the Angel lightly holding Adam with his right hand and Eve with his left. The three figures provide the main vertical lines: in a sense they are one figure, for the Angel's proportions are those of a father to stripling children and both stand or lean against him less than shoulder-high. It is not unusual for the relative size of Blake's

---

[1] Coloured drapery in *Europe* but altogether different in Tatham's copy.

figures to be symbolic or spiritual rather than realistic. There are no very marked horizontal lines in this picture except the tops of the comparatively unimportant altars which stand to right and left. The real horizontal line is an invisible one: it is the line of sight from Adam's eyes to Eve at whom he looks. Eve looks not at Adam, but with half-closed eyes downward and inward towards the Angel. The Angel looks down at both. The expression of Blake's figures and its direction should always be noted.

Plate 3, 'God Blessing the Seventh Day', has an encircling curve, as has Plate 10, 'Michael and Satan'. Commoner is the overarching curve, for which sometimes as in Plate 27, 'Satan in Council', we have an underarching curve. One might be tempted to think of this as symbolical of Hell were it nor for Plate 57, 'Ezekiel's Vision', which has two underarching curves. The curve is not always of a framework kind. In the very beautiful Plate 19, 'The Creation of Eve', a water-colour of the 1808 *Paradise Lost* series, the most striking curve is that of the sickle moon at the top of the picture. The vertical lines are supplied by the creator and Eve. He, in profile, stands holding his right arm at a slight angle above the head of Eve, who, completely created and her feet in the air just clear of Adam, faces the imaginary spectator: her hands, parted but praying, provide two more vertical lines. The creator's arm stretching across the middle of the picture is not quite horizontal, but Adam, still asleep at the base of the picture, is. The tops of the trees of the forest of this world form a slight curve across the whole picture to which the forest provides the background. The moon above is waning (too often writers on Blake fail to distinguish between waning and crescent moons, but Blake did not so fail—this is the moon of Beulah, of paradisal love, and it will not last); the creator looks with the gaze of one whose act is necessary but of twofold consequence; Eve has the rapt look of the still unsullied Emanation; Adam is asleep, his Emanation has left him and is no longer a part of him, he will have to regain her somehow.

The standing human figure with fully outstretched arms provides a vertical and a horizontal line. Blake, for whom everything living was in some sense human, hardly ever made a complete picture without figures. The figure with outstretched arms is common, the head or the head with some sort of halo or with an arch further removed providing a curve. An obvious example is 'Glad Day', first drawn in 1780 and colour-printed in 1795 (Plate 69) with a magnificent rayed background. When Blake first made this picture, it represented both the sunrise and Man (or himself) outstretched and a-tiptoe to receive the beauty and wonder of life. In his middle forties it became Albion who 'arose from where he labour'd at the Mill with slaves: Giving himself for the Nations, he danced the dance of Eternal Death'. It became sacrificial at about the time Blake was beginning to think of his *Milton*. Already in 1780 he had drawn but made no further use of a back-view of the same figure. Thirty or more years later, as Mr. Keynes has shown, this back-view is used for Albion on p. 76 of *Jerusalem*. The outstretched human figure is the crucified figure. Here, below Christ crucified on the vast tree of this world and looking up at Christ, is Albion with outstretched arms. The picture is dominated by the vertical line of Christ's body, the nearly vertical line of Albion's, the parallel horizontal lines of the two pairs of arms and the curved halo surrounding the curved crown of thorns.

One of Blake's most striking compositions is that of 'Soldiers Casting Lots for Christ's Garments' (Plate 46), a watercolour dated 1800. Here the Crucifixion is mainly in vertical lines, the centrepieces of the main cross and the two smaller ones and the large group of standing mourners. Rather dim in the background is a horizontal wall, above which appear the heads of spectators or indifferent passers-by, but the great contrast is made by the horizontal lines of the limbs of the dicing soldiers in the foreground, while their curved heads and bodies enclose them in a sphere which is both pictorially and symbolically quite disconnected from the vertical lines above them. The ideal proportions or disproportions in this picture are to be found less in the figures than in the huge crosses no Simon of Cyrene could have carried.

Reference has been made to a symbolism of right and left. This was fully developed by the time of the 'Job' series (1825) and was first discovered and expounded in 1910 by Mr. J. H. Wicksteed. Blake himself, in a notebook draft of an exposition, which was never published, of his 'Vision of the Last Judgment', wrote 'I intreat, then, that the Spectator will attend to the Hands & Feet, to the Lineaments of the Countenances; they are all descriptive of Character, & not a line is drawn without intention, & that most discriminate & particular.' The indicative, however, is not quite the same as the symbolical, which may include arbitrary but consistent conventions. Such a convention, based, no doubt, on the right and left of the scriptural sheep and goats and of the medieval Last Judgements, is used by Blake in 'Job', and there is a beginning of it at least as early as *Milton* and examples of its use in many pictures much earlier than the 'Job' series. The convention is that the right side, hand or foot, especially foot, symbolizes the spiritual, and the left the material. 'The convention, by which in the first Illustration Job's spiritual good was shown on his right hand and his material good on his left, is maintained throughout the book wherever Job is drawn in the centre.'[1] In Illustration IV Job and his wife, still concerned with material

[1] Wicksteed (1924), p. 95 and (next page) pp. 116, 16.

prosperity, both show the left foot uncovered; the messenger of disaster has his left foot and left arm forward; in the margin Satan has his left foot in advance of the other. In Illustration v, where Job gives bread to a beggar, 'the bread is both given and received with the left hand', suggesting that to neither giver nor recipient is there anything spiritual in the gift. In Illustration xix, the counterpart of v, Job and his wife are the recipients of charity ('Every one also gave him a piece of Money'). The givers use both hands, the recipients show both but stretch out neither.

In the composition of many of the 'Job' illustrations there is also a symbolism of heaven, the upper part of the picture, as 'the inner world of Job's mind, where the terrible spiritual drama is fought out between God and Satan, his own indwelling good and evil powers'. Thus in Illustration ii God sitting in heaven with the open book on his knees has the same features as Job below. This is consistent throughout the series where there is a heaven, but otherwise there are great changes. The complacent God of Illustration ii is succeeded by the disturbed one of v, by the inexorable vision of ix ('Then a Spirit passed before my face: the hair of my flesh stood up'), by the fiendlike deity of xi, by the Lord out of the whirlwind of xiii; then above God in xiv are the morning stars singing together, the instructor of xv has Job's features but a much happier expression, in xvi there is a return to ii but with the difference that Satan is now being cast down, in xvii God descends to earth and blesses Job and his wife, so that in the last four Illustrations, xviii to xxi, there is no longer a separate heaven separately depicted.

Having studied Blake's pictorial heavens in Job, we can turn back and understand the meaning of 'heavens of France' (*The French Revolution*, 206) or 'The Heavens melted from north to south' (*America*, 205) or 'the heavens of Europe' (*Europe*, 61).

Besides his colouring and composition, Blake's line must be studied. Trained as an engraver he naturally stressed the importance of line, but the experts are agreed that not until his last decade did he achieve his greatest successes with it. Then the illustrations to Thornton's *Pastorals of Virgil* (actually only the first Eclogue), the 'Job' and the 'Dante' show him a master in its use. Yet many who are not necessarily experts will find the study of Blake's line in his earlier pictures both revealing and attractive: for example, if it is true that he is not specially skilful in depicting drapery, does he not make up for that by the way in which he depicts wings of spiritual beings? There, it may be noted, his imagination was entirely free: drapery cannot escape some dependence on nature.

But for the literary student the most important line is the outline to which reference has already been made. Blake, the poet and painter of the infinite, was altogether opposed to the indefinite. He was not one of those painters who could take a brush and start somewhere in the middle of a figure, reaching the edge ultimately and somehow. His clearly imaged conceptions were as definite as could be, and his interest is in the human. One curious result of this is that clothes are often transparent or nearly so, only the edges of them making it quite clear that the figure is clothed. Thus in 'The Elohim Creating Adam' (Figgis, Plate 13), one of the colour-prints of that most fruitful year 1795, the whole of both arms and of the right leg of the creator are shown and are clothed, but the muscles of the right arm and the thigh, knee and shin are clearly visible in spite of a really substantial garment. In 'God Writing on the Tables of the Covenant', a watercolour of about 1806 (Plate 55), a filmier garment covers the whole of the back-view of the central figure but conceals nothing. Anyone can multiply examples. There are, of course, many exceptions:

some, probably all, are significant. The significance is obvious in 'The Angel of the Divine Presence Clothing Adam and Eve with Coats of Skins', since the coats of skins were intended to conceal the nakedness for which the Fall brought shame, or in 'The Angel appearing to Zacharias' (Plate 38), where Zacharias's elaborate clothing is that of his priestly office and at least as important as the man. A sub-nude Zacharias would spoil the effect of the entranced face of the man, set between priestly headdress above and the breastplate below, as it looks across at the angel of *his* annunciation. The angel's long and long-sleeved garment, on the other hand, is nearer to the usual semi-transparency.

It would be a mistake, then, to regard the cuff-line and the collar-line in Blake's pictures as merely trivial or accidental. They are boundary lines. So we never find a blurred hand or foot. Every finger or toe is distinct. If Blake had ever painted a streaked tulip, the streaks would have been clear and their number, probably, significant: 'As Poetry admits not a letter that is Insignificant, so Painting admits not a Grain of Sand or a Blade of Grass Insignificant—much less an Insignificant Blur or Mark' (MS. exposition of his 'Vision of the Last Judgment', as above).

Wordsworth once said that he had given twelve hours' thought to the condition and prospects of society for one to poetry. Blake certainly spent twelve hours thinking about pictures for one about poetry, and he passionately defended his own principles and practice against the fashions of the day, especially as those fashions had been set and expounded by Reynolds. As first President of the Royal Academy, Reynolds delivered an opening discourse on 2 January 1769. Thereafter, at first annually and then biennially, he delivered a discourse to the students at the December prize-giving, the last in December 1790. The first seven *Discourses* had appeared in book form with a dedication to the King in 1778, just before Blake was out of his apprenticeship. The first complete edition was published in 1794, two years after Reynolds's death, and contained a biography of him, but it was the second edition (1798) which Blake actually possessed. About 1808 he went through the first volume (containing the preliminary matter and the first eight *Discourses*) and annotated it with his customary vehemence. 'Having spent the Vigour of my Youth & Genius under the Opression of Sr Joshua & his Gang of Cunning Hired Knaves Without Employment & as much as could possibly be Without Bread, The Reader must Expect to Read in all my Remarks on these Books Nothing but Indignation & Resentment.' ('The Reader' suggests that Blake's remarks were intended at least for some friend to see: there is no evidence that his notes on this, or on any of the other books he annotated, were meant as preliminary to a publication.) In spite of this, about one in ten of Blake's remarks are approving, sometimes highly so, as when he writes 'These are Fine & Just Notions' against Reynolds's statement about the grand effect of the distinct colours in the draperies of the Roman and Florentine schools, or writes 'True' or 'Excellent' in other places. Reynolds, however, though he praised Michelangelo and Raphael and the 'grand style', was in practice more in the line of the Venetians and Rubens and Rembrandt. He admitted, indeed, 'that a relish for the higher excellencies of art is an acquired taste', thus—in Blake's view—giving himself away completely.

I am happy, [he annotated] I cannot say that Rafael Ever was, from my Earliest Childhood, hidden from Me. I saw & I Knew immediately the difference between Rafael & Rubens.

Some look to see the sweet Outlines
And beauteous Forms that Love does wear.
Some look to find out Patches, Paint,
Bracelets & Stays & Powder'd Hair.

So the Elijahs denounce or mock the cultured poly-
theism of the Ahabs: so the genius of the 'Mental
Prince' rages, well aware that the 'Selfhood' has
something to do with it, against the success of the men
who interpret or make the spirit of the age. 'Reynolds
. . . adds thousands to thousands', Dr. Johnson had
written. 'How much did Barry Get?' is Blake's
comment in reference to a painter he rated far higher.
When he wrote 'Gang of Cunning Hired Knaves', he
meant it: he meant the mutual benefit society of those
whose primary aim was to give the public what it could
be persuaded to pay for rather than to be obedient to
any 'Divine Vision'. The words 'Gang', 'Cunning',
'Hired', 'Knaves' can all be defended, however unfair
or one-sided the criticism may seem as a whole. Blake
drew his inspiration from far deeper and purer wells
than any of the academicians—but they were the more
civilized.

Blake's decided views on schools of painting were
expressed not only in these *marginalia*, but also in the
published *Descriptive Catalogue* of his 1809 exhibition
and in the unpublished *Public Address* (1810) on his
'Canterbury Pilgrims' picture. He could see no good
in Titian and Correggio, Rubens and Rembrandt.
He had decided against oil. In painting his own
pictures 'Clearness and precision have been the chief
objects. Clear colours unmudded by oil, and firm
and determinate lineaments unbroken by shadows,
which ought to display and not to hide form, as is the
practice of the latter schools of Italy and Flanders.' It
was not only the methods but the aims of the later
schools which he found at fault. They were naturalistic

and were therefore bound to fall short even of their lower aim. 'Men think they can Copy Nature as Correctly as I copy Imagination; this they will find Impossible, & all the Copiers or Pretended Copiers of Nature, from Rembrandt to Reynolds, Prove that Nature becomes to its Victim nothing but Blots & Blurs. Why are Copiers of Nature Incorrect, while Copiers of Imagination are Correct? this is manifest to all.' He would have liked to see the mural art of Italy revived in England: 'The Painters of England are unemploy'd in Public Works, while the Sculptors have continual & superabundant employment.' It was, perhaps, in default of this, or as leading to this, that he made his own 'invention of a portable fresco'. Of the sixteen pictures shown at his 1809 exhibition nine are such portable frescoes, the other seven being described as drawings, i.e. watercolours. Of the drawings one and of the portable frescoes four have disappeared, including 'The Ancient Britons' which one visitor at least regarded as Blake's best work. That was Seymour Kirkup, a young artist and friend of poets, a bystander later at the funerals of both Keats and Shelley, who fifty years after seeing the picture made a drawing of it for Swinburne. That too is lost.

'The Ancient Britons' has the second longest account in the *Descriptive Catalogue*. The three Britons who alone escaped in the last battle of King Arthur 'were the Strongest Man, the Beautifullest Man, and the Ugliest Man'. Had they been Greeks, they might have been Hercules, Apollo, and Pan, all understood in a strictly Blakean sense as 'the human sublime', 'the human pathetic', and 'the human reason'. The common man, as represented by Southey, thought this picture one of Blake's worst. It is lost and we cannot judge, but its symbolism is important as linking Blake's painting with his poetry, especially his later poetry. So, more subtly, does the 'Canterbury Pilgrims' picture to which not very much less than half the *Descriptive Catalogue* is devoted. 'The characters of Chaucer's Pilgrims are the characters which compose all ages and nations . . . some of the names or titles are altered by time, but the characters themselves for ever remain unaltered. . . . As Newton numbered the stars, and as Linneus numbered the plants, so Chaucer numbered the classes of men.' If this sounds unpromisingly doctrinaire, one has only to go on reading to understand how inevitable was Lamb's declaration to Crabb Robinson 'that Blake's description was the finest criticism he had ever read of Chaucer's poem'.

Blake's 'criticism' was, in a way, incidental. He was describing and explaining the details of his own picture, defending its fidelity to Chaucer and its superiority over the rival production of Stothard. Stothard's picture was full of inaccuracies—even the scene was wrong . . . 'by Dulwich Hills, which was not the way to Canterbury; but perhaps the painter thought he would give them a ride round about, because they were a burlesque set of scare-crows'. As a 'contention of friendship' this went rather far, and the evidence whether or how far these old friends eventually made it up is conflicting: but the whole description of his picture is a magnificent vindication of Blake's scheme of values. It is the 'minute particulars' that matter: there is no merely general truth. Everything that matters has meaning, i.e. is more than its superficial self. Chaucer and the twenty-nine pilgrims matter because they are the characters of all mankind. As such he has delineated and distinguished them.

These are identities. They remain essentially unchanged, but they pass through 'states'. The pictures which, more than any other, exhibited 'states' were those of 'The Last Judgment'. Of these, in addition to his design for Blair's *Grave*, Blake painted two. The smaller (1807) survives as well as a description of it by Blake in a letter. The larger and later one, described by W. M. Rossetti as '7 feet by 5 feet in dimensions, and estimated to contain 1000 figures'—a Frith's 'Derby Day' of a picture—has disappeared, but it was the subject of that manuscript (1810) addition 'to Blake's Catalogue of Pictures', to which reference has already been made. If Blake had held a second exhibition, this 'Vision of the Last Judgment' would have been included. It differs from its medieval prototypes in being symbolical. It is not individuals who are raised to heaven or cast into hell but 'states'. 'It ought to be understood that the Persons, Moses & Abraham, are not here meant, but the States Signified by those Names, the Individuals being representatives or Visions of those States as they were reveal'd to Mortal Man in the Series of Divine Revelations as they are written in the Bible.' Thus Caiaphas and Pilate are descending into the Pit, whereas Noah, Shem and Japhet (who 'represent Poetry, Painting & Music, the three Powers in Man of conversing with Paradise, which the flood did not Sweep away') are ascending to meet the Lord. This does not mean that Caiaphas is to be damned and Noah saved, but that ultimately the 'states' of selfrighteous cruelty and oppression will be cast out and the 'states' of imaginative and spiritual art exalted. Nor is this mere eschatology. 'Whenever any Individual Rejects Error & Embraces Truth, a Last Judgment passes upon that Individual.' So the individual can, in evangelical language, be saved at any time: it does not appear that he can be damned, unless, perhaps, by perpetually putting off being saved, by avoiding the Last Judgement which 'is an Overwhelming of Bad Art & Science'. Blake wrestled with this problem in *Jerusalem*. Meanwhile he painted this vast picture of the 'states' through which men could pass. 'Man Passes on, but States remain for Ever; he passes thro' them like a traveller who may as well suppose that the places he has passed thro' exist no more, as a Man may suppose that the States he has pass'd thro' Exist no more.' So, though Hell is an eternal state, there may yet be hope of emptying it: but just what Blake meant by 'eternal' and 'eternity' is a matter for later consideration. It cannot be defined in a phrase.

Blake the poet we shall see as the lyric poet, the rebel and the prophet: so the painter. In the Illuminated Books, of course, where words and pictures must harmonize, but elsewhere, too, it will help us to understand the one man if we look for these three elements— in Blake they are Tharmas, Orc who is Luvah, and Los when he has got Urizen to work under him.

Tharmas is Instinct, unfallen Tharmas is Innocence, blameless joy in a life where there is no disharmony between physical and spiritual. The most purely lyrical of Blake's pictures is 'Glad Day'—the 'Jocund day' of *Romeo and Juliet* which 'Stands tiptoe on the misty mountain tops'. The naked youth in a glory of colours is the rising sun, Apollo: he is Blake himself: he is youth standing with outstretched arms and hands, unashamed and unafraid, to receive and take his part in the loveliness of the world. Flowers open at his feet, but his eyes look straight forward to beauties being revealed by the sun which is himself. This lyric innocence Blake never wholly lost. It is to be found in remarkable passages in *The Four Zoas* and *Milton* and in such pictures as 'The River of Life', 'Jacob's Ladder', and some of the illustrations to *Paradise Lost*.

Experience succeeds Innocence. Tharmas loses his unity. Outside Eden the world is rough. Concentrated desires and emotions (Luvah) are thwarted: they take a revolutionary form (Orc). Man feels cheated: he is greater than this poor limited creature, imprisoned in Time and Space, with inadequate and contracted senses, and with his imaginative power (in which he might live) almost asleep. He is like one of Circe's animals. How, asks furious Orc, has this come about? From what miscreation do we suffer? So in 1795, at the climax of his rebel years, Blake produced 'The Elohim Creating Adam'. The background is again the sun, a vast sun with a lurid penumbra. Against this background of a Time which shuts out Eternity, 'the Elohim', winged but creating a wingless Adam, floats: one outstretched arm gathers 'the dust of the ground', the other closes in the skull of Adam, whose anguished eyes and mouth repeat, but with much greater intensity, the creator's own expression. Adam's left arm is rigidly stretched out, the flesh on his ribs is scarcely formed, and round his lower limbs, which seem to grow like a root from the ground, is wreathed the serpent whose head can not be seen. The full-grown Adam is 'Nebuchadnezzar', another colour-print of the same year. Here Blake takes the Biblical story of Nebuchadnezzar compelled to eat grass like an ox and exhibits the full horror of Circean man—man reduced to mere animal condition while the frustrated soul, which realized its fate in Adam, glares through the eyes of the man-beast and is, of course, itself perverted.

We said that Experience succeeds Innocence: it need not destroy it. Blake called them 'The Two Contrary States of the Human Soul'. The soul is, above all, Los, the Poetic Genius, the imaginative power: but the perverted soul, shut up in selfhood, takes a form which Blake called Urizen—not Apollo now but Jupiter. That way lie materialist philosophies and oppressive religions. The liberty which the imprisoned soul must somehow win is not to be found there. Yet Urizen, like Tharmas and Luvah, is an essential element in man: if only he is not allowed to usurp supreme control, this schoolmaster of souls affords indispensable help to Los, who then at last grows to full prophetic stature and produces the 'Illustrations of the Book of Job'. In the last of those Illustrations, 'So the Lord blessed the latter end of Job more than the beginning', the instruments of music, which in the first Illustration hung uselessly on the tree of this world, are all in use. The full powers of man are harmoniously employed in an enjoyment which looks beyond the mere enjoying selves. Job and his family are one in experience of innocence and in enlightenment of imagination. The setting sun and waning moon of the first Illustration are replaced by a rising sun and crescent moon. Creation was an act of mercy.

CHAPTER III

THE LYRIC POET

IF William had died in 1787 as well as Robert and if, some time in the nineteenth or twentieth century, a copy of *Poetical Sketches* had turned up and been published as an early document of the Romantic Revival, Blake might now be credited with a couple of not very well-known anthology lyrics and a varied selection of youthful imitations or experiments.

If we may presume that Blake chose the title of his own book, it was probably the painter in him that was responsible for the word 'Sketches': certainly it was the painter who wrote the now famous metaphor in *To the Evening Star*, 'And wash the dusk with silver'. The boldness of this metaphor taken from the technique of his other art is more characteristic even of this early work than is its superficial imitativeness. Phoebus may, unfortunately, have 'fir'd my vocal rage' and the auxiliary 'do' is as much overworked as by Blake's contemporaries, but to imitate the Elizabethans as in the *Song* 'My silks and fine array' was to be original: to imitate Collins or Chatterton or Macpherson or the ballads published by Percy was to choose freedom. Much of the imitation is, deliberately, at a distance. *An Imitation of Spenser* has been described by a highly competent editor as consisting of six 'successive attempts' at the Spenserian stanza 'all different and all wrong': yet even Blake could count up to nine and it is obvious that he was experimenting with variations. His seasons are Thomson's, and yet how different!

The later Blake appears here often enough to us who know him. 'Golden' is already a favourite word. He already knows his *Job*: 'the chambers of the East, The chambers of the sun' in *To the Muses* are not only Spenser's, but also derive from the 'chambers of the south' of Job ix. 9. The 'iron pen' of *The Everlasting Gospel* (derived from Jeremiah xvii. 1) is here already in the blank-verse-rhythmed prose of *Samson*. 'Albion' in *Prologue to King John* is at present only England but will become mankind in *Jerusalem*. The 'fiend hid in a cloud' of *Infant Sorrow* in *Songs of Experience* is the 'fiend in a cloud' of *Mad Song*. A line towards the end of that very Gothic poem, *Fair Elenor*, 'Hired a villain to bereave my life', reappears to one's astonishment in an epigram on Hayley which Blake confided to his notebook in London in one of his bitter hours. More important than these indications that, as in painting, so in poetry Blake used recurrent units of expression is the appearance of the enigmatic side by side with the simple. The *Song* 'How sweet I roam'd' looks simple enough, but on further consideration, since Blake did not use words unmeaningly, we are baffled by the 'sunny beams', 'silken net', and 'golden cage'. It was reserved for Northrop Frye in *Fearful Symmetry* (1947, p. 178) to resolve these enigmas in the light of *The Four Zoas*. The imagery of *To Winter* is not easy. In 'Love and harmony combine' and *Mad Song* there is no real difficulty, but there is need for the most wide-awake attention. This is no facile warbler.

Interesting and attractive as are *Poetical Sketches*, it is not there that Blake's characteristic and personal lyric note is really heard. Just as Wordsworth's *An Evening Walk* and *Descriptive Sketches* are prentice work, partly of his time and partly of himself, and acquire their chief interest because we re-examine them in the light of the work of the poet who has come into his own, while we date his real start from the first issue of *Lyrical Ballads*, so with Blake. *Songs of Innocence* (1789) are his *Lyrical Ballads*. Both aim at

and achieve simplicity, and not only in language. As
Wordsworth tried to show what is fundamental in
human nature by poems about the unsophisticated
whether young or old, a mad mother, a Betty Foy, an
old huntsman, a child of eight, so Blake opens a window
on to reality by poems about or for children, children
in years in the first place but also adult children and
then children unborn. Most of the *Songs of Innocence*
are sublime nursery rhymes. The *Introduction* shows
the piper in a wood with a flock of sheep feeding behind
him and above him a child on a cloud, who bids him
first pipe and then sing and then write:

> And I made a rural pen,
> And I stain'd the water clear,
> And I wrote my happy songs
> Every child may joy to hear.

That limpid clarity, that childlikeness which never
degenerates into childishness, comes from a perfected
early maturity. There was nothing equal to it in
Poetical Sketches.

Blake had no children, and it is only in his last
decade, when he was very happy with the Linnell
children and they with him, that we have any information about his relations with children, unless anecdotes
about his pupils and about the Astley circus boy are
considered exceptions. Children appear fairly often in
his pictures other than those which form part of *Songs
of Innocence* and the other illuminated books, but they
are not often the most striking part of the picture. There
is a notable passage in his letter to Dr. Trusler of 23
August 1799 which shows how much might have come
down to us.

But I am happy to find a Great Majority of Fellow
Mortals who can Elucidate My Visions, & Particularly
they have been Elucidated by Children, who have taken
a greater delight in contemplating my Pictures than I

even hoped. Neither Youth nor Childhood is Folly or Incapacity. Some Children are Fools & so are some Old Men. But there is a vast Majority on the side of Imagination or Spiritual Sensation.

It cannot be mere chance that the earliest published account of Blake appeared in *A Father's Memoirs of his Child* by B. H. Malkin. This book, published in 1806, has a frontispiece of the child, designed though not engraved by Blake, and contains excerpts from both *Poetical Sketches* and *Songs of Innocence*.[1] In his later 'Prophetic' books Blake speaks of 'little ones' not infrequently, though going far beyond the primary meaning, and in his great walk from Highgate down through the eastern purlieus of London (*Jerusalem* 31) he looked with pitying horror on the degradation of the guttersnipe—'the jewels of Albion' (how unlike Cornelia's !) 'running down The kennels of the streets and lanes as if they were abhorr'd'.

There was more than one school of thought about children in Blake's lifetime. There was the firm, kindly and unremitting instruction of Masters Sandford and Merton, there was a cult of nudity, there was a cult of the infant prodigy. Blake, who wrote in his notebook—

> Thank God I never was sent to school
> To be Flogd into following the Style of a Fool,

agreed with Wordsworth, who rejoiced in the liberty he had had at both home and school unlike those unfortunates who were—

> hourly watched, and noosed,
> Each in his several melancholy walk
> Stringed like a poor man's heifer at its feed,
> Led through the lanes in forlorn servitude.
> (*The Prelude*, V, 238.)

Wordsworth and Blake both believed in human innocence: it was in their reaction to experience that they

[1] And, with one variation, *The Tiger*.

differed. Blake's songs are about innocence (his use of 'of' needs constant watching to see whether the following word is subjective, objective, descriptive, possessive or genitive in the strict etymological sense): the double collection is of songs *showing* the two contrary states of the human soul, and the piper is told to pipe a song *about* a lamb. The closely packed flock of the introductory poem appears again in *The Shepherd* and again in *Spring*, where in the second picture a single lamb is detached to play with the child. So in *The Lamb* there is the flock and the single lamb in the foreground with the child, the subject of the poem being the spiritual identity of lamb, child and maker with all that that implies.

> For he calls himself a Lamb. . . .
> He became a little child:
> I a child & thou a lamb,
> We are called by his name.

'I am certain of nothing but of the Holiness of the Heart's affections, and the truth of Imagination', Keats was to write to Bailey in 1817: with 'every thing that lives is Holy' Blake concluded the *Song of Liberty* he was soon to write. In fact, however, he was, by stages, to discard the idea of holiness on earth, attacking first 'selfish holiness' and then its possibility at all. Here in the *Songs of Innocence* the idea is not expressed because it is unnecessary: there is nothing unholy with which to contrast it. In its place we have in *The Divine Image* (the only one of the *Songs of Innocence* which does not present a child or children—Adam and Eve new created take their place) a further emphasis on man's being made in the image of God, the spiritual image of course. Prayer is offered to 'Mercy Pity Peace and Love'. These are both human and divine: they are 'the human form divine'. The inclusion of the poem in a collection of songs about innocence is significant:

it ought to mean that innocence is fundamental and perhaps indestructible.

When Blake published this collection, he had not written *Songs of Experience* and no contrast with experience is exhibited. Blissful though most of the songs are, they do not exclude the 'distress' which, in *The Divine Image*, sets us praying. So there are tears in *A Dream*, in *On Another's Sorrow*, in *Night*, and even in *A Cradle Song*. There is panic as well as tears in *The Little Boy Lost*. There is experience of both thought and passion. Mr. J. H. Wicksteed, whose edition (1928) is indispensable both for its reproduction of the plates and for its interpretation, points out that songs about boys are concerned with thought and songs about girls with love. In *The Little Girl Lost* and *The Little Girl Found* this is obvious, but the beasts are surely not the passions of others but of Lyca herself. Blake uses the old notion that the lion would not attack a virgin to symbolize the harmlessness of growing up. The naked maid asleep in the cave is the innocence that will never be lost. The sorrowing parents who find her and are comforted are perhaps eventually Lyca's conscious life.

Every lyric has an occasion, an event, external or mental. Blake had been to St. Paul's Cathedral on Holy Thursday (Ascension Day)[1] and heard and seen the charity children in their coloured uniforms. He had perhaps spoken to a little sweep who was philosophical about having his head cropped. So *Infant Joy* and *The Blossom* must have had an occasion. They are poems, or a poem, of conception, feminine and masculine respectively. Mr. Wicksteed cannot be

[1] The date of the annual service was not constant during the century. From 1704 to 1728 (before it was held in St. Paul's) it was the Thursday after Whitsunday. In 1731 it was on the Thursday in the second week after Easter (29 April) and in 1750 on the Thursday in the third week after Easter (3 May).

wrong about that, though his explanation of 'two days old' as referring to the second day of the Creation may be far-fetched: it may simply mean that it is two days since, to the parents' delight, pregnancy has been established. It is certainly about that: mother and child-to-be and the announcing angel are there in the opened blossom, for the pictured blossom is part of *Infant Joy* not of *The Blossom*. Blake kept the two plates well apart in the early issues, but in the first combined issue of *Songs of Innocence and of Experience* they face one another. What was the occasion? The poems fit in too well with the disappointment which Mr. Wicksteed has suggested as the occasion of *The Book of Thel* for one to have much doubt that the Blakes in the seventh year of their married life were at last expecting a child. That was the occasion, but the subject is joy and innocence.

The Book of Thel also appeared in 1789. Though most of it is written in unrhymed fourteeners, in narrative form, mainly dialogue, and with suggestions of the prophetic, it is much more lyrical than not. Its connexion with *Songs of Innocence* is shown on the title-page, where Thel carries a shepherd's crook and watches the union of two blossoms, one feminine and one masculine (Erasmus Darwin's *Loves of the Plants* also appeared in 1789, though Blake's engraving for Darwin's work belongs to later publications, 1791, 1795 and 1799). Mr. Wicksteed suggested that Thel represents an unborn child, who, horrified by a preliminary investigation of mortal life, decides not to be born. This suggestion fails to explain the greater part of the poem and, in particular, Thel's trouble that 'Without a use this shining woman liv'd'. Thel, surely, is in this world: she laments the transience of its beauties and the failure of its apparent promises

Like dreams of infants, like a smile upon an infant's face.

She would like to fade away, but the lily of the valley, the cloud, the worm and even the clod of clay join in trying to comfort her by example and precept. She is allowed to enter the house of 'the matron Clay' and to return, not merely to 'lay me down in thy cold bed, and leave my shining lot'. So—

Thel enter'd in and saw the secrets of the land unknown.
She saw the couches of the dead, and where the fibrous roots
Of every heart on earth infixes deep its restless twists:
A land of sorrow and of tears where never smile was seen.

Finally she came 'to her own grave-plot' and heard from it a 'voice of sorrow' asking vainly the reasons for the self-treachery of the life of the senses. Then—

The Virgin started from her seat, and with a shriek
Fled back unhinder'd till she came into the vales of Har.

She was the Mistress and the Beauty and the Queen of the vales of Har. That was where she belonged. This woman (her name could be derived from the second syllable of Catherine) has had cause for deep despondency: to be shown, very beautifully, how to get outside herself was not enough: she had to come very near to spiritual death and to fly from it in horror. The couches are those of the spiritually dead, and the grave-plot is like those in *The Garden of Love* which Blake was soon to write and include in *Songs of Experience*. In this poem four gentle lyrics fail to release Thel from the Giant Despair. She would like—

Sleepe after toile, port after stormie seas,

or, as she puts it—

And gentle sleep the sleep of death, and gentle hear the voice
Of him that walketh in the garden in the evening time.

It takes the authentic voice of Despair in his true character to make her 'arise, and leave this cursed place'.

Songs of Experience was advertised by Blake on 10 October 1793, but no copy of that issue survives. In 1794 the combined *Songs of Innocence and of Experience* were published, if that word is not misleading. To the new *Experience* collection Blake transferred from *Innocence* the double poem *The Little Girl Lost* and *The Little Girl Found* and, in later issues, *The School-boy*.[1] All the rest but four (*Introduction, Ah! Sun-flower, A Little Girl Lost,* and *To Tirzah*) are a selection of eighteen from about sixty poems, whole or fragmentary, written on the last eight leaves (reversed) of the notebook which had once been Robert's.[2] Blake was not a professional poet and this small amount of heartfelt lyric cannot possibly have been spread evenly over the four years 1789–93. One does not write this sort of poetry like that, but in something resembling 'the continuous excitement under which in the early months of 1895' Housman wrote *A Shropshire Lad.* It was probably a continuous excitement in the early months of 1793 that produced *Songs of Experience.* Certainly the first written, *My Pretty Rosetree,* was occasioned by, and records, a marital misunderstanding. A very attractive woman had made advances to Blake, which, as a happily married man, he had rejected. Coming home, very pleased with himself, he told his wife. Instead of praising him for his fidelity, she was angry and jealous because he had thought the other woman attractive. The tension lasted some time, as is evident from some of the poems Blake did not publish, but before the summer all was well. Blake fell in love again with Catherine and records it in a poem he did not publish—*The Fairy,* which he at

---

[1] He also in the first issue of the double collection included *Laughing Song* in both halves.   [2] The "Rossetti MS."

first called *The Marriage Ring*. If I am right in thinking these poems all belong to a few months and were not spread over years, it follows that some biographers have tended to make too much of the few poems which testify to a quite temporary trouble.

Yet this trouble may have had something to do with the 'continuous excitement'. So had two other things which happened in February 1793, the outbreak of war with France and the publication of Godwin's *Political Justice*. Blake certainly knew Godwin already, but this book could harm him as it harmed Wordsworth. Godwin attacked marriage at a time when Blake was uncomfortable at home and Godwin disbelieved in emotional virtues such as gratitude and pity. So quite early in this new outburst of lyrics Blake wrote of an Angel and a Devil who disagreed about Mercy and Pity. This is the first poem which directly challenges one of the *Songs of Innocence*. Later on he rehandled the subject in the poem which he finally named *The Human Abstract*, the opposite at all points of *The Divine Image*. He went on to *Infant Sorrow*, the opposite of *Infant Joy*: to expect a baby is delightful; to be one is another matter. In *London* the streets are wintry,[1] be it noted. After it comes *The Lilly*, which is perhaps the lily-of-the-valley as in *Thel*. Then comes *The Tyger*, the occasion of which is not known, but the importance Blake attached to it is shown by the fact that the poem as he wrote it with numerous changes is followed by a fair (though not final) copy. Two pages further on comes the first verse of *The Chimney Sweeper*, 'A little black thing among the snow'.[2] There was very little snow in London in the first half of 1793. It snowed on 12 March at night; a very little fell on 28 March; on 1 April (Easter Monday) it snowed 'without intermission till 4 p.m.', according to the *Gentleman's Magazine*. Perhaps it

[1] In the MS.   [2] See Plate I.

NURSES Song

When the voices of children are heard on the green
And whisprings are in the dale:
The days of my youth rise fresh in my mind,
My face turns green and pale.

Then come home my children, the sun is gone down
And the dews of night arise
Your spring & your day, are wasted in play
And your winter and night in disguise.

From SONGS OF EXPERIENCE

Same size as original design

was then that Blake saw the child. Two more verses were added three pages later to *The Chimney Sweeper* but the snow was over: he had 'smil'd among the winter's snow'. *Holy Thursday* comes later on the same page. We cannot be certain that this was occasioned by an actual attendance at the service in St. Paul's as was the first poem of that name. Blake was by now well aware that he was writing, had indeed nearly finished, a series of songs of Experience: the first *Holy Thursday* was in part the occasion of the second. Ascension Day in 1793 was, however, on 10 May, which would be close on the warm weather of the next poem, the last used, *The Fly*. Composed still later, and not in the notebook, was *Ah! Sunflower*.

The frontispiece of *Songs of Experience* depicts the piper of the *Innocence* frontispiece with the same flock behind him in a more open landscape: but he has no pipe and, instead of looking up to a child in a cloud, he looks straight forward and supports on his head a winged and wide-eyed cherub whose outstretched arms he holds in his uplifted hands. He has a look of intense, almost tragic, seriousness. The titlepage to *Experience* shows a father and mother stretched out in death and two mourning daughters (Blake's mother died in 1792). In about half the poems children still appear. Very striking are in *Nurses Song* the boy enduring to have his hair combed[1] (this has a tremendous development in the human sacrifice carried out by females in *Jerusalem* 66), in *London* the small child who insists on instructing Aged Ignorance, in *The Chimney Sweeper* the quite wonderful picture of the 'little black thing' in the snowstorm before daybreak: the sky is as black as his garments and soot-bags.[2] *A Little Girl Lost* and *A Little Boy Lost* represent respectively youthful, not literally childish, love and thought, which crash against authority, which, even if right, uses only authoritarian

[1] See Plate II.   [2] See Plate I.

methods: 'the maiden bright' is crushed not by force or even reason but by the 'loving look', the tyrannous appeal to the affections: the little boy who, like Tom Paine, sincerely and courageously proclaims most un-Blakean doctrine, is persecuted in exactly the spirit of those who burnt heretics at the stake.

It is in these *Songs* that Blake the rebel achieves his finest lyrical expression:

> Children of the future Age,
> Reading this indignant page;
> Know that in a former time,
> Love! sweet Love! was thought a crime.

But the next chapter will be the right place for considering some of its subject-matter. Not, however, all. There is no rebellion in *The Lilly*, the third member of the little trilogy on a single page, which shows the three stages of the matrimonial trouble—quarrel, wistful tension, reconciliation. *The Tyger* is a poem of acceptance, as later (Illustration 15) Job accepts Behemoth and Leviathan. *To Tirzah*, written after the poems from the Rossetti MS.,[1] has got past the antithesis of Innocence and Experience to a new antithesis, mortal and spiritual. Tirzah was the capital for several reigns of the northern kingdom of Israel in contradistinction to Jerusalem, the capital of the southern kingdom of Judah. Not for a few years do Blake's extant writings use Jerusalem as a name for the spiritual, though it is implicit in his use here of Tirzah, but he knew Galatians iv. 26: 'Jerusalem which is above is free, which is the mother of us all.' Tirzah is 'Mother of my Mortal Part', and, as Jesus said to his mother, 'What have I to do with thee?' In the *pieta* at the foot of the page the mortal part of Jesus is attended unavailingly by the two Maries, but Joseph of Arimathea (preacher of the gospel in Britain and subject of two other of Blake's

[1] Perhaps much later, but I incline to think not.

pictures) proffers what is probably the water of life and has 'It is Raised a Spiritual Body' inscribed on his robe. 'The Death of Jesus set me free.' Blake was to spend twenty-five years working out the full implication of that, and in 1818 *Jerusalem* was finished.

Blake's poetry had passed the stage of innocent assertion or childlike question ('Little Lamb who made thee?') and had reached that of a different sort of question. *The Tyger* as Blake punctuated it contains fourteen question marks (not in the MS., but Blake like others composed with little or no punctuation). Those are questions of the startled imagination. It is noteworthy that, except for *Earth's Answer*, all the other poems appearing for the first time in *Songs of Experience* and containing questions were written after *The Tyger*: they include the four successive questions of indignant pity in *Holy Thursday*, the two of *The Chimney Sweeper* ('Where are thy father & mother? say?'), the last line of *A Little Boy Lost*, the rhetorical and repeated 'What have I to do with thee?' of *To Tirzah* and, perhaps last written, the pleading 'Why wilt thou turn away?' of *Introduction*.

The frequent question and the lyrical note are both found in *Visions of the Daughters of Albion*, which was also ready for sale by 10 October 1793. Blake here went back to the unrhymed fourteeners of *The Book of Thel* but with a vigour that is not without violence. In *Europe* (1794) there are also lyric passages, especially in its rejected preface beginning 'Five windows light the cavern'd Man'. The grim *Book of Urizen* and its Lambeth successors contain little or nothing that can be called lyrical except Ahania's lament. We come to unpublished poetry, especially *The Four Zoas* and the contents of the Pickering MS.

The Pickering MS. (so-called because in 1866 it belonged to someone of that name) contains fair copies of ten poems. It is pretty certain that they were composed during the Felpham period and the accepted date of the MS. is 1803. It is not a fair copy prepared for publication, for there is no punctuation and some of the couplets and quatrains of the longest poem *Auguries of Innocence* must be out of their proper order. Moreover, publication of mere letterpress without pictorial accompaniment was not Blake's habit. Still the making of this set of fair copies must indicate that Blake thought the poems more important than many of the rough or fugitive pieces which he wrote when in the mood. They are all poems of experience but of an experience which does not end with but starts from *To Tirzah*: the lyric poet has become the prophet. An attempt will be made in a later chapter to indicate more fully what this means. The vision of Eternity which had come to Blake, 'the Divine Vision' which he and his wife kept in time of trouble, provided no facile material for art whether pictorial or poetic. Of these ten poems the apparently simplest are *The Land of Dreams, Mary, Long John Brown & Little Mary Bell*, and *William Bond*. In *The Land of Dreams* it would be tempting to identify Thomas with little Thomas Malkin,[1] who died in 1802, but his mother survived him and that precludes that literal interpretation: the Mother ('of my Mortal Part') is innocent Nature, a 'Land of Dreams' not of reality, the Father is organized society in its most kindly aspect (but it cannot 'get to the other side'), the child wants to get away from 'this Land of unbelief and fear'. That is a beautiful dream: it is not the solution to the problem. *Mary* may well have been occasioned by reflection on the life and death of Mary Wollstonecraft, but Blake applied two lines in it to himself: the troubles of conscious genius and those of unashamed beauty and charm are two examples of a single truth. Blake trying to conform at Felpham 'went out in Morning attir'd plain & neat'. *Long*

[1] See p. 52.

John Brown & Little Mary Bell (of which the first verse should be printed as a preamble or summary) deals on the surface with the miseries of chastity, enforced on the one side, contumacious on the other, but this is also a parable or symbol of the rejection of Imagination. *William Bond* shows the triumph in Love of selfless Imagination with no hint of deceit of self or others.

> Seek Love in the Pity of others' Woe,
> In the gentle relief of another's care,
> In the darkness of night & the Winter's Snow,
> In the naked & outcast, seek Love there!

The Grey Monk is more than a poem on the miseries of war and the futility of a war to end war: it enounces a fundamental doctrine of Blake's that, if Satan is used to cast out Satan, Satan still rules:

> The iron hand crush'd the Tyrant's head,
> And became a Tyrant in his Stead.

Blake, quite as much as the Lake poets, recognized that violence and other deadly sins had made the French Revolution a failure. 'The Sensual and the Dark rebel in vain', wrote Coleridge in 1798.

The Smile, with its faulty syntax, is perhaps a not very successful attempt to lead up to the Divine Vision. Three poems, *The Golden Net*, *The Mental Traveller* and *The Crystal Cabinet*, have a good deal in common. *The Golden Net* harks back, but with a vast difference, to 'How sweet I roam'd' in *Poetical Sketches* where 'the prince of love'—

> caught me in his silken net,
> And shut me in his golden cage.

Then the boy Blake was still semi-conventional. Now the man is concerned in these three poems with the attractiveness and the balefulness of the 'Mother of my Mortal part'. The 'Three Virgins', the 'Woman Old' and the 'Maiden' respectively lure under a net, chain to a rock and imprison a masculine soul. In *The Golden Net* he is beguiled by the irresistible smile of natural beauty which cannot satisfy: desires must be ungratified: 'when will the morning rise?' In *The Mental Traveller*, which is cyclic and in parts very difficult, the masculine soul breaks his chains and for a time uses and dominates the female who has now become 'a Virgin bright': but after this union or compromise he becomes old and poor and finally, after taking a maiden in his arms as David took Abishag, is beguiled by her and 'her sweet smile' to infancy. He is born again as at the beginning of the poem, and she becomes the 'Woman Old'.

> She nails him down upon the Rock,
> And all is done as I have told.

This, like *The Grey Monk*, is a poem of the wrong solution. *The Crystal Cabinet* also ends with a birth. Again there is a compelling smile. Certainly the poem is, at one level, a poem of the pre-natal life: the unborn babe lives in Beulah: it is his attempt to 'seize the inmost Form' which results in his birth.

> A weeping Babe upon the wild,
> And Weeping Woman pale reclin'd,
> And in the outward air again
> I fill'd with woes the passing Wind.

He has awakened from the false but lovely dream. What next? The Divine Vision?

Auguries of Innocence is Blake's own teasing title. It is in the octosyllabic couplets which he wrote easily and sometimes rather badly and pairs with the 'Proverbs of Hell' in *The Marriage of Heaven and Hell* as a gnomic collection. It should be read in the Oxford editor's rearrangement or rather arrangement, for Blake's copying out was obviously not in an order in

which he would have published. It is quite possible
that the title properly belongs only to the famous
introductory quatrain ('To see a World in a Grain of
Sand'). The section following extends to all animals
the intense feeling manifest in 'the dog at the wintry
door' of Enion's wail in *The Four Zoas*, and the whole
poem breathes Blake's profound belief in souls, not
systems, and in the power of the soul to reach inward
to the Human-Divine. The first apprehension of God
is one of light in darkness, but, as we grow at ease in
Eden, we realize that we are made in his image.

> God appears, & God is light,
> To those poor souls who dwell in Night:
> But does a Human Form Display
> To those who Dwell in Realms of Day.

To much the same time as the Pickering MS. poems
belong the forty-four octosyllabic couplets of the
famous poem sent to Butts with a letter of 22 November
1802 and written, said Blake, 'above a twelvemonth
ago' ('With happiness stretch'd across the hills'). It
describes one action in the great mental battle that
went on at Felpham—to stay or return? It is of
primary importance for Blake's symbolism: the thistle
is both a physical obstruction and a type of 'Aged
Ignorance' and prudential worldliness, and the sun is
both the literal lord of physical life and 'Los the
terrible', the Poetic Genius, who warns of the inevitable
effect in time of a fatal step. It concludes with Blake's
defiance. He transcends the physical.

> Now I a fourfold vision see,
> And a fourfold vision is given to me;
> 'Tis fourfold in my supreme delight,
> And threefold in soft Beulah's night,
> And twofold Always. May God us keep
> From Single vision, & Newton's sleep!

Fourfold vision is, among other things, vision exercised by all the four Zoas in integrated harmony. *The Four Zoas* is in the main far from being a lyric poem, but, like *Milton* and even *Jerusalem*, it has its lyric passages, many more in fact. An unpublished and ultimately abandoned poem, it probably belongs to the years 1797–1803, to Lambeth and Felpham, before the penultimate grimness of South Molton Street. The MS. was written and revised in more minds than one, but the number of lyrical or quasi-lyrical passages is considerable, nor is their beauty to be passed over. Much of the dramatic dialogue of this poem is conducted in songs in which the fourteeners are smoother than is usually found in the narrative. Yet even the narrative can be lyrical:

The Earth spread forth her table wide; the Night, a
    silver cup
Fill'd with the wine of anguish, waited at the golden
    feast.
But the bright Sun was not as yet: he, filling all the
    expanse,
Slept as a bird in the blue shell that soon shall burst
    away.

                          (II 89–92; I Keynes.)

Night II is, indeed, full of such passages. There are Enion's two laments. The first (II 187–202; I Keynes) opens with—

Why does the Raven cry aloud and no eye pities her?

and runs through the sorrows of bird and beast down to insect—

The Spider sits in his labour'd Web eager watching for
    the Fly:
Presently comes a famish'd Bird, & takes away the
    Spider.
His Web is left all desolate that his little anxious heart
So careful wove & spread it out with sighs & weariness.

The second (II 595–626) contrasts the ease of thoughtless joy in prosperity with the bitter cost of experience:

What is the price of Experience? do men buy it for a
     song,
Or wisdom for a dance in the street? No! It is bought
     with the price
Of all that a man hath—his house, his wife, his children.
Wisdom is sold in the desolate market where none come
     to buy,
And in the wither'd field where the farmer plows for
     bread in vain.

That is preceded by Enitharmon's song of the triumph of woman:

Arise, you little glancing wings & sing your infant joy!
Arise & drink your bliss!
For every thing that lives is holy; for the source of life
Descends to be a weeping babe.

Night v ends with 'The Woes of Urizen'. He laments his great mistake and its dire results:

O did I keep the horses of the day in silver pastures?
O I refus'd the lord of day the horses of his prince!
O did I close my treasuries with roofs of solid stone,
And darken all my Palace walls with envyings & hate!

In Night IX there is a long passage (386–554) of an Arcadian sweetness and simplicity which describes the happiness of Luvah and Vala 'in lower Paradise'. It is young love, Eden and innocence restored, 'for the Eternal Man is Risen'. It is a happier *Book of Thel*, with Thel no longer lonely or despairing.

'I am not here alone; my flocks, you are my brethren;
And you birds, that sing & adorn the sky, you are my
     sisters'. . . .

Then Luvah pass'd by & saw the sinless Soul
And said: 'Let a pleasant house arise to be the dwelling
place
Of this immortal spirit growing in lower Paradise!'

The Four Zoas ends in lyrical happiness that has come
after experience.

The Sun has left his blackness & has found a fresher
morning;
And the mild morn rejoices in the clear & cloudless
night.
And Man walks forth from the midst of the fires: the
evil is all consum'd.

'How is it we have walk'd thro' fires, & yet are not
consum'd?
How is it that all things are chang'd, even as in ancient
time?'

The poetry of *Milton* opens with the lyric now
commonly called 'Jerusalem'.

And did those feet in ancient time
Walk upon England's mountains green?

Jerusalem shall be rebuilt. 'For Zion's sake will I not
hold my peace and for Jerusalem's sake I will not
rest. . . . And give him [the Lord] no rest, till he estab-
lish, and till he make Jerusalem a praise in the earth'
(Isaiah lxii). So Blake would 'not cease from Mental
Fight' and swung the strange two-handed engine called
Milton. Much of it is anything but lyrical, yet one
notes Blake once again (it started in *The Book of Thel*)
singing of the humblest creatures (I 24; 29 Keynes),
insects and weeds, and in Book II (31; 34 Keynes) we
have the birds and flowers.

Thou hearest the Nightingale begin the Song of Spring.
The Lark, sitting upon his earthly bed, just as the morn

Appears, listens silent; then, springing from the waving
    Corn-field, loud
He leads the Choir of Day, trill! trill! trill! trill!
. . . first the Wild Thyme
And Meadow-sweet, downy & soft, waving among the
    reeds,
Light springing on the air, lead the sweet Dance; they
    wake
The Honeysuckle sleeping on the Oak; the flaunting
    beauty
Revels upon the wind; the White-thorn, lovely May,
Opens her many lovely eyes. Listening, the Rose still
    sleeps;
None dare to wake her: soon she bursts her crimson
    curtain'd bed
And comes forth in the majesty of Beauty. Every Flower,
The Pink, the Jessamine, the Wall-flower, the Car-
    nation,
The Jonquil, the mild Lilly, opens her heavens; every Tree
And Flower & Herb soon fill the air with an innumerable
    Dance,
Yet all in order sweet & lovely. Men are sick with Love.

Each of the four chapters of *Jerusalem* opens with
prose and lyric, the third lyric being the remainder of
the poem from which *The Grey Monk* in the Pickering
MS. was carved. Two stanzas are repeated from *The
Grey Monk*, one of which concludes the third *Jerusalem*
poem:

    For a Tear is an Intellectual thing;
    And a Sigh is the Sword of an Angel King;
      And the bitter groan of a Martyr's woe
    Is an Arrow from the Almightie's Bow.

The introduction to the fourth chapter takes up the
theme of that to the second and of 'Jerusalem' in *Milton*:

    And now the time returns again:
      Our souls exult, & London's towers
    Recieve the Lamb of God to dwell
      In England's green & pleasant bowers.

Elsewhere in *Jerusalem* we shall find few lyrical touches. Exceptions are in the strange and beautiful Joseph and Mary episode (pp. 61, 62) and in some of the triumphant closing passages, such as Los's song (pp. 85, 86) and the final call to Jerusalem (p. 97):

Awake, Awake, Jerusalem! O lovely Emanation of
    Albion,
Awake, and overspread all Nations as in Ancient Time!
For lo! the Night of Death is past and the Eternal Day
Appears upon our Hills. Awake, Jerusalem, and come
    away.

Blake's lyric gift never left him. Look at 'Job', Illustration XIV, where the Morning Stars sing together, or Illustration XXI, where Job and his family play upon all instruments of music whereof the lyre is one.

CHAPTER IV

THE REBEL

IF it is true, as Gilchrist said, that in June 1780 Blake was caught up in the mob of Gordon rioters and carried on to witness the storming of Newgate, it did not make a revolutionary of him: even so Wordsworth passed through France in 1790 almost untouched by political enthusiasm. It was the fall of the Bastille not of Newgate which for a while made a revolutionary of Blake. In the years between he had at times an 'unbending deportment', but, so far as writing is concerned, his recalcitrance shows itself mainly in a fantastic and lighthearted satire—and unfinished and unpublished at that. *An Island in the Moon* (Blake's rough MS. in the Fitzwilliam Museum has no title, but it begins 'In the Moon is a certain Island') was unknown until the present century and is often dismissed as unlike and unworthy of Blake. It forgets the Moon almost at once, but, as Dr. Blackstone makes clear in *English Blake*, the Moon was suggested by the Lunar Society of Birmingham whose members, like many of the characters in Blake's satire, were scientists who met (once a month) in each other's houses in turn: some of the characters can be identified, e.g. Inflammable Gass is Priestley and Etruscan Column is Wedgwood. Blake came across these people in London and he went himself to similar meetings, e.g. at the Mathews' house, though he had left that salon by 1787, the probable date of *An Island in the Moon*. Yet there, as here, we know that conversation was interspersed with song: and here, in Chapter 11, where the meeting is at the house of Steelyard the Lawgiver (possibly Godwin, for this rigid lawgiver objects to lawgiving, 'said that it was a shameful thing that acts of Parliament should be in a free state'), the fatuousness is suddenly dispersed by the first version of three of the *Songs of Innocence*, sung by three different characters. This MS., as the Rossetti MS. does for most of *Songs of Experience*, shows the actual composition of these three songs, *Holy Thursday*, *Nurse's Song* and *The Little Boy Lost*. After that the fatuousness never quite recovered itself. Part of the following MS. has been lost, but it ends with an early reference to what was to become Blake's Illuminated Printing and with a conversation containing a significant mention of 'that noble beast the Tyger'.

Blake's satire or burlesque, which reaches backward to Swift and forward to Peacock or even, in Chapter 5, to Lewis Carroll, is interesting in many ways. The first chapter is concerned with Voltaire: was he 'a fool' or 'the Glory of France'? (Wordsworth, we remember, found him dull.) Chatterton is discussed with utter ignorance at one meeting: at another 'Chatterton never writ those poems'. Steelyard takes extracts from Hervey's *Meditations among the Tombs* and Young's *Night Thoughts*, both of which were to inspire pictures by Blake. One fatuous subject of discussion is whether Pindar was a better poet than Giotto was a painter. The women have their own particular fatuousness, and Mrs. Sinagain is a good name. The songs are of all sorts. The surgeon is horribly callous, but there is a limit: 'I do it because I like it. . . . I think, somehow, I'll leave it off. There was a woman having her cancer cut, and she shriek'd so that I was quite sick.' The scientific experiment in Chapter 10 is a fiasco.

Blake did not pursue this method. It did not go deep enough for him. Perhaps the only line of sheer burlesque in a prophetic book is *The Four Zoas*, III, 156, where Tharmas, who among other things is god of the sea, exclaims in the true 'shiver my timbers' vein of the sailorman—

Fury in my limbs! destruction in my bones and marrow!

Otherwise the elements in *An Island in the Moon*, which Blake rejected for use in either of his arts, found their outlet in *marginalia* and above all in epigram and other doggerel verse, of which some has survived in the Rossetti MS. Here we find the lurking satirist, perhaps cynic, who sees the so different thoughts that accompany the conversational word. Here survives that very slight scatology which yet seems to take us straight back to Swift and Pope. Here, somewhat soured, is that sense of fun which is so obvious in *An Island in the Moon*. 'Fun I love, but too much Fun is of all things the most loathsome', he wrote in 1799 to Dr. Trusler. In fact *An Island in the Moon* is lacking in the 'wirey bounding line' which Blake considered essential to a work of art.

Giving up the way of burlesque satire, the rebel in Blake turned, probably in 1788, to epic narrative. The three to four hundred fourteeners of *Tiriel* are an attack on 'Aged Ignorance' and the whole method of human upbringing. Imagination and instinct are suppressed: the father 'scourges off all youthful fancies'. The educator is a hypocrite and the greatest sufferer from his own errors. For Tiriel is Lear. As Blake wrote later in *The Gates of Paradise*:

> In Vain-glory hatcht & nurst,
> By double Spectres Self Accurst,
> My Son! my Son! thou treatest me
> But as I have instructed thee.

Here Tiriel curses his sons: 'Serpents, not sons' ('How sharper than a serpent's tooth it is to have a thankless

F

child !', *Lear*, I, iv, 309, but Blake has in mind also the serpents who destroyed Laocoön). He has accursed daughters too. He has tyrannized over his uncivilized brothers. Blind and age-bent he wanders over the world. He gets back to an insipid simplicity where he cannot stay. He recognizes himself as both the child and father of error.

Compell'd to pray repugnant & to humble the immortal
    spirit
Till I am subtil as a serpent in a paradise.

Then the serpent-father of serpent-sons falls dead.

With this too Blake was dissatisfied. He made an interim fair copy, with some corrections, and he drew what would have been twelve full-page illustrations. These have been dispersed. The MS. is in the British Museum.

For publication he went back largely to satire. Strangely enough, it was rebellion against a recent enthusiasm of his own, for Swedenborg, which stirred him to write, illustrate, and publish *The Marriage of Heaven and Hell.* Swedenborg's 'writings are the linen clothes folded up', the grave clothes for which the risen man has no further use. An internal date fixes the beginning of this work. Swedenborg's 'new heaven' began in 1757, the year of Blake's birth, 'and it is now thirty-three years since its advent'. Therefore 'The Eternal Hell revives. And lo ! Swedenborg is the Angel sitting at the tomb'. Jesus was thirty-three at his Crucifixion. Swedenborg is an 'Angel', but the mood of *The Marriage of Heaven and Hell* is satire—it deals with 'what the religious call Good & Evil'. The religious with whom Blake had had most to do in this year 1790 and the year before were the Swedenborgians. He had carefully read the 1788 English translation of Swedenborg's *Wisdom of Angels concern-*

ing Divine Love and Divine Wisdom and made many annotations in his copy, most of them favourable: one of them contrasts Swedenborg's teaching on one point with what 'was asserted in the society'. Two comments, 'Good & Evil are here both Good & the two contraries Married' and 'Heaven & Hell are born together', are the germs of *The Marriage of Heaven and Hell*. Similarly, Blake read and made annotations in the 1790 translation of Swedenborg's *Wisdom of Angels concerning Divine Providence*. He made some very unfavourable comments on Swedenborg's predestinarianism. 'Cursed Folly!' The *Wisdom of Angels*, and Swedenborg an Angel: so *The Marriage of Heaven and Hell* is a satire on Angels. The easiest way to read it without missing the point is to think of 'Angel', 'Devil', 'Heaven', 'Hell', 'Good', and 'Evil' as always in quotation marks—'what the religious call Good & Evil', what you call 'Hell' or the 'Devil'. I think otherwise, I think you shallow conformists, so afraid of energy and imagination, are stigmatizing as 'infernal' the most vital part of man. There is a storm coming.

> Rintrah roars & shakes his fires in the burden'd air;
>   Hungry clouds swag on the deep.

Once there was the energy and imagination and endurance that created Christianity. Now it has all been made smooth and conventional: the worldly find it very comfortable. Those in whom the spirit of the pioneer Christians survives rage in the wilderness outside. There is a storm coming.

That is 'The Argument', but the work goes on with a Swedenborgian title (*Heaven and Hell*, translated 1778, was one of his works) and with each chapter of exposition followed by 'A Memorable Fancy' in mockery of Swedenborg's method of Memorable Relations.

The title-page shows two figures embracing in the fires under the earth: the marriage can only be celebrated in 'Hell'. So on the 'Argument' page an energetic figure in a tree strains down to clasp the hand of, or perhaps to hand a fruit to (but the tree is no apple-tree), another less enterprising figure standing on the ground. At the head of the work proper is energy itself in the form of fire (the human figure in the fire is fire itself, for everything that lives is not only holy but human): the result is the new birth depicted at the foot of the page. In contrast with the fire which 'delights in its form' is the chained and straining figure in the fire at the foot of the next page. Here is energy chained, desire ungratified, imagination blinded. Worse, he would like to get into his clutches the babe recently born who has, just in time, been caught by a free spirit in the light of the rising sun. Later on Blake worked up this design and made a colourprint which he called 'The Good and Evil Angels', the words not, of course, being used in the special sense of *The Marriage of Heaven and Hell*. Energy chained becomes perverted (''Tis against that', Blake, like Beaupuy, might have said, 'that we are fighting'). Satan with sword, horse, chariot, and the very sun and moon falls, on the next page, into the Miltonic Hell: desire restrained 'becomes . . . only the shadow of desire. The history of this is written in Paradise Lost'. Now Blake, having seen through Swedenborg's 'Wisdom of Angels', will 'shew the nature of Infernal wisdom' in a series of Proverbs of 'Hell', preceded by the now famous couplet warning against the blinded imagination:

How do you know but ev'ry Bird that cuts the airy
     way,
Is an immense world of delight, clos'd by your senses
     five?

At the end of the Proverbs of imaginative energy is an amusing picture of the 'Devil' (surely a lamb in wolf's clothing, the Poetic Genius not so very diabolical and with Blake's own fiery hair) eagerly pointing to his unrolled scroll of proverbs which an industrious lady on his right (perhaps the standing figure of the 'Argument' page) is copying down, while an equally industrious lady on his left leans across to see it too. So the pictorial accompaniment goes on. To read the bare, unaccompanied text is like reading the words of a song in ignorance of the music. The last picture, like the fifth, he worked up later for a colour-print. It is of Nebuchadnezzar and illustrates the Proverb of 'Hell' that 'One Law for the Lion & Ox is Oppression', a succinct statement of the flaming individualism of the book. The leonine monarch compelled to 'eat grass as oxen'!

The open rebellion against Swedenborg reaches its height in the last chapter. He had no originality. He did some easy exposing of religious hypocrisy and thought he was 'the single one on earth that ever broke a net [of religion]'. He is like a man who 'carried a monkey about for a shew, & because he was a little wiser than the monkey, grew vain, and conciev'd himself as much wiser than seven men'. 'Swedenborg has not written one new truth . . . he has written all the old falshoods.' Why? Because he did not attempt to get into the mind of 'Devils'. In the appended Memorable Fancy an 'Angel' and 'Devil' argue. The latter claims Jesus as the great exemplar of Infernal Wisdom: 'Jesus was all virtue, and acted from impulse, not from rules.' Then follows the Marriage. The 'Angel' embraced the 'Devil' in his 'flame of fire & he was consumed and arose as Elijah'. In a marriage of Reason and Energy, Energy will be in command, and the result will be a Prophet whom many will think a devil, as Ahab must often have thought Elijah. Later he will be equated with the Poetic Genius, Los, who 'is the Spirit of Prophecy, the ever apparent Elias' (*Milton*, 23[71]).

The Marriage of Heaven and Hell bears its own internal date (1790). It has no date on the title-page, but was included in the list of 10 October 1793. Blake went on producing copies. One of those extant, that in the Fitzwilliam Museum, was made very near the end of his life. We should, therefore, assume that its opinions remained his, even if we had no other writings to corroborate. He acquired some important ideas from Swedenborg,[1] but his differences remained. The 'Devil's' statement about Jesus not living by rules is amplified in the unpublished *Everlasting Gospel*, probably written as late as 1818.

Attached to *The Marriage of Heaven and Hell* was *A Song of Liberty*, a short prose-poem of revolution, political, moral and religious. There is no disillusion about it. A greater than Swedenborg has come. Later he will be called Orc. So Blake settled down to write an epic of *The French Revolution* in Seven Books. Johnson was to publish in the ordinary way. The 306 lines of Book I got as far as page-proof with a title-page dated 1791, but nothing more happened. Perhaps Johnson took fright, and wisely so. The page-proof eventually became Linnell's property. It was first published in 1913 in the Oxford *Blake*.[2] 'The remaining Books of this Poem are finished, and will be published in their Order' runs an Advertisement in the page-proof. Even as early as 1791 'finished' may with Blake have meant finished in his mind, as nine years later 'In my Brain are studies & Chambers filled with books & pictures of old, which I wrote & painted in ages of Eternity before my mortal life'. It is quite possible

---

[1] The best account is in Chapter III of J. G. Davies, *The Theology of William Blake*.

[2] Oxford Standard Authors series.

that Blake, having seen the page-proof of Book i, took
a dislike to publishing in that unilluminated form and
let it go as he had *Poetical Sketches*. It is noteworthy
that the proof, which bears the publisher's but not the
author's name, has not a single author's correction. Did
Blake not get as far as that? Or was the copy we have a
spare one? The modern editors have corrected a few
obvious misprints, but there may well be more,
especially of punctuation and quotation marks: in one
place (after line 241) it looks as if a line has dropped out.

The seven-beat metre of *Tiriel* and *The Book of Thel*
is used, but with an anapaestic basis, and it is often hard
to count as few as seven beats. In its cloudy way it
can be very effective. There are far more similes than
is usual with Blake.

Sudden as the bullet wrapp'd in his fire, when brazen
    cannons rage in the field,
Fayette sprung from his seat saying 'Ready'. Then
    bowing like clouds, man toward man, the Assembly
Like a Council of Ardours seated in clouds, bending
    over the cities of men,
And over the armies of strife, where their children are
    marshalled together to battle,
They murmuring divide; while the wind sleeps beneath,
    and the numbers are counted in silence,
While they vote the removal of War, and the pestilence
    weighs his red wings in the sky.

There in six lines are three similes, but in the last line
is the symbol-metaphor which is so much more Blake's
normal use.

The history is not exactly that of the historians. One
of the Bastille prisoners is the Man in the Iron Mask
who actually died in 1703. The strong man is Duke of
Burgundy, but there was no such Duke. There are no
base passions or petty motives on either side. The
awfulness of the passing of a historic order and a

historic religion is set against the brave new world. It
is a change like that in Keats's *Hyperion*, where Oceanus
can ask—

> Have ye beheld the young God of the Seas,
> My dispossessor? Have ye seen his face?

So Orleans asks his fellow-nobles:

> Have you never seen Fayette's forehead, or Mirabeau's
>   eyes, or the shoulders of Target,
> Or Bailly the strong foot of France, or Clermont the
>   terrible voice, and your robes
> Still retain their own crimson?—Mine never yet faded,
>   for fire delights in its form!

It is in fact the purifying fire of imagination, the return
to primal freedom and spiritual power, that is the
justification and aim of this rebellion. It was no mere
matter of politics or economics or social justice. It
was the undoing of the Fall.

> When the heavens were seal'd with a stone, and the
>   terrible sun clos'd in an orb, and the moon
> Rent from the nations, and each star appointed for
>   watchers of night,
> The millions of spirits immortal were bound in the ruins
>   of sulphur heaven
> To wander enslav'd; black, depress'd in dark ignorance,
>   kept in awe with the whip
> To worship terrors, bred from the blood of revenge and
>   breath of desire
> In bestial forms, or more terrible men; till the dawn of
>   our peaceful morning,
> Till dawn, till morning, till the breaking of clouds, and
>   swelling of winds, and the universal voice;
> Till man raise his darken'd limbs out of the caves of
>   night. His eyes and his heart
> Expand—Where is Space? where, O Sun, is thy dwel-
>   ling? where thy tent, O faint slumb'rous Moon?

None felt the bliss of that dawn more ardently than Blake. It is no wonder that he felt the inadequacy of Swedenborg who had only conversed with 'Angels'. A shock of disillusion came quickly enough, but he had felt the bliss and, in a sense, it was permanent.

Diverted, for whatever reason, from continuing with *The French Revolution*, Blake turned back to its predecessor and progenitor, the American Revolution. *America* is called 'A Prophecy' (the only other poem so called is *Europe*) in the sense not of a prediction but of an exposition of fundamental spiritual principles. Like *The French Revolution* it introduces historical persons and deals with a historical event, but there are new characters of a different kind—Orc and Urizen. The names are new (Orcus and Urian Zeus), but they are the 'Hell' and 'Heaven' of *The Marriage of Heaven and Hell* and the 'new-born terror' and 'starry king' of its appendage, *A Song of Liberty*. To keep up after *The Marriage of Heaven and Hell* the ironical use of so many terms would have been impossible:[1] so a new nomenclature begins. *America* is the first of the 'prophetic' books. The new mythology and terminology is to grow and change for twenty-five years. Overlapping of old and new conceptions will sometimes make for obscurity.

Fragments of older 'myths' overlap the new one. No one can say when Blake first created for himself a coherent imaginary world. As the Quincey children did and as the Brontë children did, so perhaps did young William Blake, though he would be more likely to draw than to describe his country of the mind. At any rate in his early maturity his day-dreams had taken the form of such a country. The Land of Har is the scene of *Tiriel*. *The Book of Thel* is episodic to it: it reappears

---

[1] In line 217 the old use remains, an indication that *America* was not written so long after *The Marriage of Heaven and Hell*.

for a moment in *The Song of Los*. It is not allegory, but imaginative fiction or mythopoea. 'Meaning' or application comes later, for the creating imagination knows more than the surface mind. Another such day-dream dealt with the lost Atlantis. Under the ocean that 'Golden World' still existed. A fragment of this myth finds its way into *America*, but we cannot hope to know more of the unwritten story of Herodotean Ariston 'the King of Beauty' and 'his stolen bride'. Ariston reappears in *The Song of Los*.

So much hard and ingenious work has been put into the interpretation of Blake's 'symbols' that one is in danger of forgetting that they are never mere symbols and never started as symbols. They started as part of a story or they started as pictures. How often must his powerful visual imagination have projected on to the paper a picture of which he did not at first understand the full meaning. 'Glad Day' after years becomes Albion. He copies an unimportant figure from the edge of a Michelangelo print: then he calls it Joseph of Arimathea: after years it becomes 'One of the Gothic Artists who built the Cathedrals'. He makes a design —of a vast chained figure, of an old man entering a dark door, of a young man looking upward—and uses it, or a variant of it, over and over again as he finds more 'meaning' in it. Certainly he illustrated his books (and other books): certainly the words of *Songs of Experience* preceded the pictures: but one must always be prepared to take a picture as a starting-point of 'meaning' and not as a mere illustration or symbolic presentation. At the head of the Preludium to *America* is a picture of a boy chained to the ground: a man and a woman stand by him in deep distress. The boy is Orc. The man and woman will, in a later poem, be identified as Los and Enitharmon. We do not know whether Blake had yet made that identification when he designed *America*. He did not say so, and if, with our superior knowledge, we say 'those two are Los and Enitharmon, his parents' and leave it at that, we run away from the 'meaning'. Orc we know—desire, energy, imagination—and we should see the 'Prophecy' starting with Orc chained and Man and Woman in misery at that: he may be their child, but they have lost him.

America, perhaps begun in 1792, was one of the works advertised on 10 October 1793 and the title-page bears the date 1793. It had '18 designs': in fact the 263 lines of text (including 37 of Preludium) are almost the junior partner. The anapaests of *The French Revolution* have gone: so, strangely, has some of the sublimity: but the central idea is the same, that this is no mere political rebellion but the saving for Earth of a 'portion of the Infinite'. The debate of *The French Revolution* goes on. It is the debate inaugurated with irony in *The Marriage of Heaven and Hell*. On one side is Albion's Angel, on the other the Angels of the thirteen colonies. These are not the 'Angels' of *The Marriage of Heaven and Hell*, but 'mental deities' like the 'angels of the seven churches of Asia' in Revelation from which Blake borrowed them. If he drew them, they would be 'spiritual forms'. Albion's Angel takes his stand 'beside the Stone of night', that is the double-stoned table of the ten commandments which were inscribed in the literal and symbolic darkness of Sinai. Albion's Angel, the spirit of the British government, takes the line of restrictive law (nine of the ten commandments are prohibitions), of justice (for oneself), of rights. For him the voice of freedom and resurrection and hope is the voice of the devil, of Orc who is a—

Blasphemous Demon, Antichrist, hater of Dignities,
Lover of wild rebellion, and transgressor of God's law.

Orc accepts the challenge with a touch of the irony of *The Marriage of Heaven and Hell*:

I am Orc, wreath'd round the accursèd tree.
The times are ended; shadows pass; the morning 'gins
　　to break.
The fiery joy that Urizen perverted to ten commands,
What time he led the starry hosts thro' the wide wilder-
　　ness,
That stony law I stamp to dust, and scatter religion
　　abroad
To the four winds as a torn book, & none shall gather
　　the leaves.

Blake's rebellion against religion was clear enough in
The Marriage of Heaven and Hell. In *The French
Revolution* the Archbishop of Paris had his terrible
dream of the end of religion and how 'God, so long
worshipp'd, departs as a lamp Without oil'. Now Blake
has found a name for the god he wants to abolish, the
god of most religious people: it is Urizen. He really
exists—'in the human breast'.

To Orc's outrageous defiance of authority Albion's
Angel replies by threatening war and appealing to the
loyalty of the colonists.

Sound! sound! my loud war-trumpets, & alarm my
　　Thirteen Angels!

But the thirteen are 'burning with the fires of Orc'—in
fact, they are Orc, since he too exists only 'in the human
breast'. Boston's Angel takes the lead in rejecting
Urizenic authority and hypocrisy:

What God is he writes laws of peace, & clothes him in a
　　tempest?

The Revolution breaks out. The war, the real war
against the religion and morality of Urizen, is not at
first universally successful. Not for twelve years did
France receive 'the Demon's light'.

BOSTON'S ANGEL FLYING THROUGH THE DARK NIGHT

From AMERICA

Perhaps, in view of the proclamation against seditious writings (May 1792), it was as well that Blake confined himself to 'Illuminated Printing'. Once more the designs are an integral part of the poem. It is a complete mistake to call them 'decorations' or to think that they tell a different but parallel story. They illustrate the text. Sometimes this is obvious as in the picture of Urizen anxiously listening to Orc's outburst or in that of Boston's Angel exultantly borne 'thro' the dark night' on a flying swan[1] (so much learning and ingenuity has gone to the misinterpretation of some of the pictures in Blake's books that it is really important to remember that 'Particularly they have been Elucidated by Children'), or in the 'dragon form' of 'Albion's wrathful Prince' or, at the bottom of the same page, in the spiritual form of George III tearing his hair:

The King of England, looking westward, trembles at the vision.

Sometimes the pictures amplify the text. Very striking is that which is drawn above, beside and below the few lines beginning 'Albion's Angel stood beside the Stone of night'. One human figure holds up another ready to throw him down. On one side of him a human figure draws the sword of justice, on the other side another holds the scales, of which one side tips down. Below it the figure thrown down from above is seen falling into hell-fire, and beyond, the same figure falls into the coils of a serpent. This is the justice based on your current religion and morality, on 'the Stone of night'. This is the punishment which sends to hell instead of redeeming, for these flames are not the flames of Orc. Similarly, the religion, against which Blake, perhaps not altogether wrongly and

---

[1] See Plate III.

certainly not altogether rightly, imagined the Americans to have rebelled, is shown on a later page as a woman with outstretched hand instructing a docile youth, while parallel to her hand is a serpent with outstretched fang: instruction and threat of punishment are simultaneous.

Sometimes the pictures amplify the text almost in the sense of supplying a missing passage. Below line 141, the outbreak of the Revolution, is the often-used design of Death's Door: the Revolution is the death of the old life. Below the challenge of Albion's Angel to Orc is a ram against whose sides two children sleep. The 'terrific form' in which Orc appears is not his only form: his is the way to Arcadian innocence.

Immediately after the decisive declaration of Boston's Angel is the design, already used in *The Book of Thel*, of children riding a lightly-bridled serpent who is obviously enjoying himself too. Again it is Orc (not Urizen) who can lead man to innocent happiness. The serpent, it will be noted, has in *America* no intrinsic or consistent symbolic meaning. Here, no doubt, he is suggested by the Isaian asp.

America was followed by *Europe* (1794) and *Africa* and *Asia*, the last two forming the content of *The Song of Los* (1795). As in *America* Blake went back to what preceded the French Revolution, so in *Europe* he went back to what preceded the American Revolution, right back to the birth of Jesus. In the Preludium are heard the groaning and travailing of natural life, life which lives upon death and is melancholy with its own deathwish. This is the same shadowy (i.e. phenomenal) female who in the Preludium to *America* fed Orc till Orc was ripe for her. She wants a redeemer from the torture of mere phenomenal life. How is that to be?

And who shall bind the infinite with an eternal band
To compass it with swaddling bands?

The last two words come not from the Bible but from Milton's *On the Morning of Christ's Nativity*. So *Europe* proper starts from that poem. 'The deep of winter', 'secret', 'eternal day', 'War ceas'd', 'crystal house', 'peaceful night' leave no doubt. In Milton Jesus was born, war stopped, the angels sang, the heathen gods fled. In Blake Jesus was born, war stopped for the occasion, Los and Enitharmon separately sang songs very different from that of the angels, and Enitharmon summoned sons and daughters who seem much like the heathen gods under odd aliases. Los, the poetic genius, is 'possessor of the moon', he is far from real enlightenment: peace and plenty, wine and song, that is what Los would like the 'Prince of Peace' to mean, that and nothing more. He can keep Orc in his place, too. Enitharmon, the eternal feminine, pervades the physical universe. It is perhaps the 'winds of Enitharmon' which blow the long white hair and beard of 'The Ancient of Days', which is the frontispiece to *Europe*. She also pervades human society. Her song on the night rather than morning of Christ's nativity begins—

Now comes the night of Enitharmon's joy.
Who shall I call? Who shall I send,
That Woman, lovely Woman, may have dominion?

More subtly than the Wife of Bath she will have mastery. She will give 'Woman's love' all the attraction of the forbidden. 'Forbid all Joy' (note the capital letter) '& from her childhood shall the little female Spread nets in every secret path'. Blake had been reading Mary Wollstonecraft's *Vindication of the Rights of Women*, which attacks coyness and coquetry. War and Priesthood and the Nunnery are all products of Enitharmon and will help her design. For eighteen hundred years she slept. Los and Enitharmon, Man and Woman, blighted what might have been the harvest of Christianity. They can be seen in Blake's picture doing it deliberately. War is continuous, but Enitharmon's dream jumps to the American War and what caused it—the serpent religion which is as old as Avebury and as recent as Bacon. The coiled but threatening serpent on the title-page, the serpent whose coils extend up the side of the page which describes the visit of Albion's Angel to the 'ancient temple serpent-form'd', is often called the serpent of materialism, and that is near enough. 'Thought changed the infinite to a serpent.' It is quite the wrong symbol for eternity. On the contrary it is 'shut up in finite revolutions'. Only a 'philosophy of the five senses' could make such a mistake:

and man became an Angel,
Heaven a mighty circle turning, God a tyrant crown d.

So Blake the rebel attacks the whole foundation of Church and State, the 'ideology' which made possible the American war. In the southern porch of the serpent-temple is 'the Stone of Night' which we already know from *America*.

Albion's Angel rose upon the Stone of Night.
He saw Urizen on the Atlantic,
And his brazen Book,
That Kings & Priests had copied on Earth,
Expanded from North to South.

The supreme embodiment of priestcraft is the Pope, and there he sits, a permanent manifestation of Urizen. The Lord George Gordon anti-Popery riots were 'flames of Orc', but the war-propaganda went on and

Enitharmon laugh'd in her sleep to see (O woman's
    triumph!)
Every house a den, every man bound. . . .
Over the doors 'Thou shalt not', & over the chimneys
    'Fear' is written.

There is a Bastille.

Enitharmon is awakened and continues her song,
but soon day comes and with it the French Revolution.
She is 'in anguish and dismay', but Los 'call'd all his
sons to the strife of blood'.

With the magnificent exceptions of the frontispiece
and the Preludium picture of the assassin lying in wait
for the pilgrim, *Europe* is inferior to *America*, which
Foster Damon calls the most splendid of all Blake's
prophecies. There are some fine lines and impressive
descriptions, the free-verse songs vary the fourteeners,
but it is full of obscurities from the beginning. It is
clear that Blake is attacking current Christianity and
civilization, but his attitude to 'the secret child' himself
is curiously unclear. Some of the pictures are much
cruder than those in America, e.g. War between two
Angels of Peace is mere allegory without 'Vision'.

As *America* went behind *The French Revolution* and
Europe went behind *America*, so *Africa* goes behind
Europe. It goes back to the beginning of the Laws of
Urizen, which were given 'to the Nations By the hands
of the children of Los'. So early began *la trahison des
clercs*: the men of art and letters used their powers to
impose on men's minds those undiscriminating laws
which are the same for the Ox and the Lion. They
found for them an 'abstract' philosophic basis in India
and in Greece, and 'Moses beheld upon Mount Sinai
forms of dark delusion'. The misguided asceticism of
John the Baptist was passed on to Jesus. Christianity
meant monasteries. Mohammedanism and the Goths
were two forms of reaction against that. Legalism

G

means all sorts of futile ways to try 'to catch the joys of Eternity', but they are not to be snared by 'Churches, Hospitals, Castles, Palaces'. The sense of 'Eternity' was lost when legalism and asceticism began. Then man and woman became

> narrow doleful forms
> Creeping in reptile flesh upon
> The bosom of the ground;
> And all the vast of Nature shrunk
> Before their shrunken eyes.

The process went on

Till a Philosophy of Five Senses was complete.
Urizen wept & gave it into the hands of Newton & Locke.

The heavy clouds of 'The Argument' to *The Marriage of Heaven and Hell* hang over Europe, Asia, and Africa, and this short poem of 52 lines ends with a repetition of the first line of *America* proper. It brings the history up to that point.

The reason for the title *Africa* is not obvious, though the song is sung by Los in 'heart-formed Africa' and in it Orc is a Prometheus chained on Mount Atlas. The 66 lines of *Asia* may be so called to finish the round of the continents or as a matter of precaution, for the 'Kings of Asia', whose object is to keep their subjects submissive by poverty and pestilence, are not distinguishable from the kings of Europe, and the kings of Europe are not distinguishable from the government of George III. *Asia* is a bitter attack on what Blake took to be current economic theory and practice, including the fixing of wages (1795 was, in fact, a difficult year, the year in which the system of family allowances known as the Speenhamland scale began). It all comes from that fundamental wrongmindedness called Urizen, from Christianity as we understand it. Adam,

Noah, and (in *Africa*) Ariston symbolize states of happiness that have been and could be again, but—

> Adam, a mouldering skeleton,
> Lay bleach'd on the garden of Eden;
> And Noah, as white as snow,
> On the mountains of Ararat.

Then Blake dashes into prophecy of the future. Revolution will bring Resurrection.

This is very sudden. We don't see how or why. Neither did Blake. The rebel had not yet fully graduated into the prophet. That is why the series of Lambeth books, for all their struggling power and vivid but bounded vision, seems to peter out. This deficiency is apparent in most of what has still to be considered of the output of these remarkable years 1792–5, *Visions of the Daughters of Albion* with the related poems of *Songs of Experience* and *The Book of Urizen* with its two sequels. An exception is *The Gates of Paradise* which has next to no words. This, described as 'a small book of Engravings. Price 3*s*.', is in the list of 10 October 1793. The title-page and plates are dated 17 May 1793. Sketches for all the plates are found in the Rossetti MS. The fact that that MS. book was in use for sketching in the early months of 1793 is an additional reason for thinking that the *Songs of Experience* were written then. The title-page describes the book as *For Children*. It has none of the verses added later and should, at this stage, be examined in its original form of seventeen emblems and titles only. The emblems start before birth and end after death: they almost but not quite tell a continuous story. They are of great vigour and imaginative intensity, yet with an economy and simplicity of expression which might well lead to their being 'Elucidated by Children'. The tree, the vegetation, which already in both picture and poetry ('Tyger! Tyger! burning bright In the forests of the night') symbolizes this material and perishing world, appears in several, sometimes as a background, more often overhanging. 'What is Man?' is asked of the chrysalis-form of the frontispiece. From the merely natural point of view he seems to come from the earth like the mandrakes for which Rachel bargained with Leah, the world of the mere four elements. He sits under a branch which does not shelter him from the downpour: he is shown almost imprisoned in earth in one of several claustrophobic pictures Blake made in these years: the expanse of air and cloud and stars makes him brood but not understand: the fiery energies have no purpose or direction. The young and happy spirit is like a short-lived butterfly which a lout knocks down with his hat. Youth is brutal to Age, but Age, too, has relied on brute force. At one moment Man is longing for the Moon, at the next and in consequence he cries for help as he drowns. Age in its folly clips the wings of Youth and teaches the damnable doctrine of a God who punishes vindictively, the sort of God who could deliberately starve Ugolino and his children. The opposite is the truth— the gate to Paradise. The death of one who means much to us (as Robert did to William) brings fear and hope, it opens the eyes of our spiritual imagination to see beyond this phenomenal world. One whose eyes are so opened will not delay. He will die to this world which ends with the worm as it began with the caterpillar.

Visions of the Daughters of Albion is also in the list of 10 October 1793. Its title-page does not bear the word 'Lambeth', which may mean that it was published early in the year before Blake's removal: in that case it must be the work of 1792 and probably preceded *America*, which does say, 'Lambeth'. The omission need not, however, be significant, and it is more likely both that *America* was written next after *The French Revolution* and that *Visions of the Daughters of Albion* was written after the publication of Mary Wollstone-craft's book and concurrently with *Songs of Experience*.

'Albion' is merely England or rather Britain, 'the island white', and not, as in *Jerusalem*, a synonym for Man. The biblical form of phrase 'Daughters of Albion' explains itself, but, as so often in Blake, the meaning of 'of' calls for consideration. Do the Daughters see or are they seen in the Visions? They appear as a woebegone group in two of the pictures and (lines 1, 43, 113, 218) they provide a chorus of sympathizers for Oothoon. The poem describes what they see: 'of' is subjective.

The poem has been very differently interpreted—as a mere variation on the eternal triangle and a proclamation of sexual libertinism or as a spiritual myth. The pictures do not add quite as much to the text as usual. It is clear, however, that there are three 'visions', each ended by the line, 'The Daughters of Albion hear her woes & echo back her sighs'. 'The Argument' covers only the first vision (lines 1–43). It is natural to take Oothoon's plucking of the flower as symbolizing sexual experience in the physical sense, but in fact the vision is easier to understand if the plucking of the flower means falling deeply in love—Blake is always concerned with what goes on in the soul. Oothoon then 'over Theotormon's reign took her impetuous course'. Then came the disaster with Bromion—

> the terrible thunders tore
> My virgin mantle in twain.

Bromion threw her aside. Theotormon ('God-tormented'?) can neither give her up nor take her: for him she is for ever chained 'back to back' to Bromion. Oothoon, if she needed purifying, is purified by the

righteous anger of Theotormon and her own acceptance of it.

> The Eagles at her call descend & rend their bleeding
>   prey.
> Theotormon severely smiles; her soul reflects the
>   smile,
> As the clear spring, mudded with feet of beasts, grows
>   pure & smiles.

So ends the first vision. It is certainly easiest to take
the three characters as actual individuals. In the
second vision the scene is still the cave of Bromion on
the threshold of which Theotormon sits weeping, but
Oothoon is no longer bound back to back to Bromion.
Though chained by the feet, perhaps to Bromion, she
'hovers' by Theotormon's side (text) and above him
(picture) 'persuading him in vain'.

>   Arise, my Theotormon! I am pure,
> Because the night is gone that clos'd me in its deadly
>   black.

The 'deadly black' is the world of the mere five
senses, the world of the materialist in which Oothoon
had for a time been sunk. She has got beyond that and
calls Theotormon, whose pure image she reflects, to
'turn his lovèd eyes' upon her. Theotormon remains
in despair: he asks doubtingly about this comfort of the
life of the spirit. Bromion, in a later poem described
as 'loving Science', interposes undoubtingly: there is
only nature with its laws, 'one law for both the lion
and the ox'.

In this second vision we seem to be getting away from
the individuals. The hovering of Oothoon above
Theotormon means, in Blake's practice, the approach,
successful or not, of a new state of mind. He came to
use this form of visual symbol often enough, e.g.

Jerusalem 71¹ 'above Albion's land was seen the Heavenly Canaan'. Oothoon, who passed from innocence to dark experience and has now escaped into a new marriage of innocence with experience, rejects Bromion and accepts Theotormon's moral standards, which should, however, now be absorbed in the new life of the soul emancipated from the mere senses. The vision now seen by the Daughters of Albion is one of spiritual struggle and resistance.

In the third and last vision any hope of integration which we may have formed during the second is shattered. Theotormon's purity is seen to be Urizenic. It is based not on a realization that 'everything that lives is holy', but on the law of prohibition. This sort of chastity Oothoon rejects. It is the cause of loveless marriages and of most miserable sexual perversions and irregularities: Theotormon is seen scourging himself. It leads, too, to the 'hypocrite modesty' of the man-catching woman.

Then is Oothoon a whore indeed! and all the virgin
    joys
Of life are harlots; and Theotormon is a sick man's
    dream,
And Oothoon is the crafty slave of selfish holiness.

She rejects that sort of femininity. Instincts are to be satisfied, not repressed with all the Freudian consequences of repression. Love is to be free, but not possessive.

I cry: Love! Love! Love! happy, happy Love! free
    as the mountain wind!
Can that be Love that drinks another as a sponge drinks
    water,
That clouds with jealousy his nights, with weepings all
    the day?

Let us live openly and freely, in the life of the spirit and of the body.

Bromion has disappeared in this vision, but Theotormon is unconvinced. He remains sitting 'Upon the margin'd ocean, conversing with shadows dire'.

It is all very well for us, with a century and a half of intermittent hope and disillusion behind us, to smile at the naïveté of these revolutionary visions. Oothoon is pure love, Theotormon becomes impure from his over-purity, Bromion—is left out. It is easy, too, to stress too much or too little the libertinism of the third vision. Blake's own life was, even by the strictest Urizenic standards, blameless. He had a horror of prostitution, its causes and effects:

> But most thro' midnight streets I hear
> How the youthful Harlot's curse
> Blasts the new-born Infant's tear,
> And blights with plagues the Marriage hearse.
> (*London*, in *Songs of Experience*)

He believed, with St. Paul, that the law, i.e. prohibition, makes sin. He believed, with St. Paul, that 'the greatest of these is Love'. He believed—and this was his strength, but few are as strong as Blake—that (to use a terminology foreign to him) *agape* and *eros* must fuse. In that fusion is the lovers' paradise so ecstatically sung by Oothoon. There is no mere vulgar libertinism: one notices how both here and in *Songs of Experience* (*A Little Girl Lost*) this 'free love' is feminine.

The attack on mere 'chastity' is continuous in Blake. It is true that the word comes to have very wide connotations, but the essential point is its negativeness: it is identical with 'pale religious letchery' (*America* 68). 'Whosoever looketh on a woman to lust after her hath committed adultery with her already in his heart', St. Matthew v. 28, and *King Lear*, IV, vi.—

Thou rascal beadle, hold thy bloody hand!
Why dost thou lash that whore? Strip thine own back:
Thou hotly lusts to use her in that kind
For which thou whipp'st her.

This nursing of unacted desires (better strangle them
at birth than nurse them unacted) comes from
'chastity', from prohibition. The religion of love has
reverted to Sinai. So in *Songs of Experience*—

I went to the Garden of Love,
And saw what I never had seen:
A Chapel was built in the Midst,
Where I used to play on the green.

And the gates of this Chapel were shut,
And 'Thou shalt not' writ over the door;
So I turn'd to the Garden of Love,
That so many sweet flowers bore.

And I saw it was filled with graves,
And tomb-stones where flowers should be;
And priests in black gowns were walking their rounds,
And binding with briars my joys and desires.

Man was made for joys, not for the priestly sabbath.
Wordsworth and Coleridge said the same. Wordsworth wrote of 'the grand elementary principle of
pleasure' and of 'joy in widest commonalty spread':
Coleridge—

Joy, William, is the spirit and the power,
Which, wedding Nature to us, gives in dower
    A new Earth and new Heaven,
Undreamt of by the sensual and the proud—
Joy is the sweet voice, Joy the luminous cloud—
    We in ourselves rejoice !
And thence flows all that charms or ear or sight,
    All melodies the echoes of that voice,
All colours a suffusion from that light.

'The Church', on the other hand, in *The Little Vagabond*, 'is cold' in contrast with the Ale-house with its ale and 'pleasant fire'. Of course 'Kings and Priests' was a revolutionary catchword, not always used intelligently, like 'capitalist' in the twentieth century. Blake says little about kings except in *Asia*, but the priest at this time was certainly a *bête noire* to him, as is shown unreservedly in the Papal picture in *Europe*. After a few years he dropped the priest and searched deeper.

He was, indeed, searching much deeper already. No sexual ethic can stand *in vacuo*. Blake was well aware of that, as *Visions of the Daughters of Albion* shows: his interpreters should always be aware of that awareness. Searching deeper, Blake came, with startling results, to the Fall—the Fall and the Creation, including the creation of Woman. *The First Book of Urizen* (but there was no other and later it is called simply *The Book of Urizen*) is Blake's *Genesis* and *Paradise Lost*. It was a beginning, no doubt, of that 'Bible of Hell' promised in *The Marriage of Heaven and Hell*. The Preludium tells us that it concerns 'the primeval Priest's assum'd power'. Urizen is that Priest as opposed to Los, who, with all his imperfections, is the eternal Prophet.

We know from Milton and, less coherently, from the Bible of two Falls—the Fall of the Angels and the Fall of Man. In Milton the Creation comes between these two. The newly-created world was to make up for Heaven's loss of the rebel angels, but the rebel angels scored a victory by bringing about the second Fall. There are three orders of spiritual beings—God, Angels, Man. For Blake, however, the spiritual world is essentially one. A Fall is a disruption, a disintegration of that spiritual unity. Blake will not have Milton's account. He rebelled against Milton consistently. Finally, he had to write *Milton* to make Milton put himself right. The Bible cannot be wrong, but it can be wrongly interpreted. It is for the prophet to give the right interpretation and show where the religion of the priests has gone wrong.

The title-page shows the seated hunched-up figure of Urizen with his snowy (and therefore cold) flowing hair and vast beard: his hands stretch to right and left and hold pens: above him bends the vegetation of this world: behind him are the two tables of the law looking remarkably like the tombstones which they are. In front of him protrudes, on his left, one bare foot—a right foot: the right foot, the foot of spirituality, is misplaced, and just in that consists the Fall. We must remember that Urizen, like Satan, had his original glory. The Fall of Urizen is in a sense the Fall of God: having fallen he was Satan but is still worshipped as God. Blake says this over and over again. It is precisely his quarrel with what passed as Christianity in his day and before his day. Much later he sums it up in *The Everlasting Gospel* in the antithesis between Caiaphas and Christ—Caiaphas, the moral priest, who worshipped Satan and thought him God, and Christ, who knew that we cannot use Satan to cast out Satan.

At the head of the first of the nine chapters of *The Book of Urizen* is a striding figure with arms outstretched against a fiery mass, inwards to which his head is turned. This is the poet-prophet looking fearlessly into the flames of Orc and prepared to receive 'dark visions of torment'. Torment starts with Chaos: Chaos came from Urizen's original act of self-separation from the eternal family. He wished to be self-sufficient, solitary—it is as near to the traditional Pride by which the angels fell as makes no matter. He did not draw a third part of heaven after him, nor was he punished. His act of isolation created 'a shadow of horror', Chaos. Blake's Chaos is the 'without form and

void' of the Bible and the Chaos of *Paradise Lost* and
of the beginning of Ovid's *Metamorphoses* (Blake was
'very fond of Ovid', says Tatham) but with a most
significant difference. Blake was incapable of accepting
or indeed understanding un-souled matter. Chaos could
only be the expression of a Chaos-soul. This first
terrific chapter, with its visual and spiritual imagery of
dark conflicts and wild and transient appearances,
describes the Soul in Chaos, the immediate consequence of the first Fall. An uneven three-beat blank
verse has taken the place of the fourteeners of the
previous books.

> Times on times he divided & measur'd
> Space by space in his ninefold darkness,
> Unseen, unknown; changes appear'd
> Like desolate mountains, rifted furious
> By the black winds of perturbation . . .
>   . . . voices of terror
> Are heard, like thunders of autumn
> When the cloud blazes over the harvest.

'Darkness was upon the face of the deep' (Genesis),
but the 'brooding' (*Paradise Lost*, VII, 236) of 'the
spirit . . . on the face of the waters' was the 'brooding
secret' of this dark, unprolific, self-closed Eternal
named Urizen.

There is no creation in this first chapter, though
Urizen 'self-contemplating' in his 'abominable void'
throws up, as it were, anticipations of what is to be.
Chapter II opens with a quite definite statement—

> Earth was not, nor globes of attraction.

So Ovid explains that no Sun, Moon, or Earth existed
in the primeval chaos. They could not exist, Blake
explains, for—

The will of the Immortal expanded.
Or contracted his all flexible senses;
Death was not, but eternal life sprung.

Sun, Moon, and Earth exist only for beings whose
senses have lost their flexibility and are limited to a
mere five. Urizen had not yet sunk as low as that,
though his terrible mistake will lead to it. He is per-
sistent. He sounds what one may call the First Trump.
In Milton's Hell the fallen angels reassembled 'at the
warlike sound of Trumpets loud': here it is the 'myriads
of Eternity' who had not fallen who 'muster around the
bleak deserts' to hear Urizen's proclamation. He is the
only one in step. He is holy and 'hidden': in chaos he
has—

> sought for a joy without pain,
> For a solid without fluctuation.

As Milton's Satan fought his way through Chaos—

> Into this wilde Abyss,
> The Womb of nature and perhaps her grave,
> Of neither Sea, nor Shore, nor Air, nor Fire,
> But all these in their frequent causes mixt
> Confus'dly—
>
> (*Paradise Lost*, 11, 910–14)

so Urizen in 'Nature's wide womb' claims to have
struggled successfully, to have reached, and to be, dry
land. The conquerer of Chaos must achieve Cosmos:
Urizen has thought it all out and written it in his
solitude in 'the Book of eternal brass'. As a disordered
nation seeks comfort in a despotism, so the soul of
Chaos finds refuge in a Procrustean tyranny.

> One command, one joy, one desire,
> One curse, one weight, one measure,
> One King, one God, one Law.

The Eternals had at first avoided the 'petrific abominable chaos', then they came to hear what Urizen had to say, now at that terrible Act of Uniformity they fix a great gulf between him and them.

> Eternity roll'd wide apart.
> Wide asunder rolling;
> Mountainous, all around
> Departing, departing, departing,
> Leaving ruinous fragments of life
> Hanging, frowning cliffs, &, all between,
> An ocean of voidness unfathomable.

It was not done as a punishment like the casting of Satan into Milton's Hell. It was an inevitable part of Urizen's rejection of the free and unsequestered energies of Eternity. The fires of those very energies, in so far as they reach Urizen, produce now no light but rather darkness visible, and burn with 'fierce anguish'. The Urizenic soul has to escape from them and protect itself like a troglodyte. Against the heat of Eternity, Urizen built himself a strong universe—a 'black globe' it seemed to the 'sons of Eternity' (an 'opacous Globe', *Paradise Lost*, III, 418)—and, as the Cherubim were set to keep Paradise clear of Adam and Eve, Los had to keep watch 'to confine the obscure separation alone'.

At this point it is as well to remind ourselves what is happening. Just as from *The French Revolution* Blake worked step by step backwards through *America*, *Europe*, and *Africa*, so in *The Book of Urizen* he set out to find the origin and fundamental nature of the Urizenic spirit which he found ruling and being worshipped in the world. Blake was not attempting to get 'Beyond Good and Evil': no one can do that: the man who thinks he can is merely substituting his own conception of Good and Evil for the current one: that was

what Blake was doing. The current versions of the
Fall did not make sense: they were, in fact, Urizenic
propaganda. The real spiritual truth about the Fall
must have been as here related—withdrawal into self,
chaos, the mistaken cosmos of a sick, mad soul. When
Blake reached the point of the final separation of
Urizen's world from Eternity, he could not forget that
Urizen's world, that is our world, has nevertheless
some link with Eternity. We are not utterly cut off,
though often we seem to be so. That link must be the
power of poetry and prophecy, which he called Los,
whom we have already met, not altogether at his best,
in *Europe* and *Africa*. The conception of Urizen
should now be clear and his subsequent activities in
this book should cause no difficulty, but Los will need
careful study.

The mathematical-logical-legalistic self-contemplating Urizen and the poet-prophet fashioner into form,
Los, have hitherto been one. Now Los is made
Urizen's keeper: the two suffer a 'wrenching apart'.
Los falls: though imagination and energy are his
('intense fires for his dwelling'), there is 'a fathomless
void for his feet' and he howls with the pain of the
wrenching until it heals. But Urizen's wrenching did
not heal and he lay 'in a stony sleep, Unorganiz'd, rent
from Eternity'. Los takes fright at the 'direful changes'
which go on in the apparently dead Urizen.

Spiritual, as opposed to phenomenal, creation comes
about by division. Los is divided off from Urizen,
Enitharmon from Los, Orc from Enitharmon. Each
division, whatever the value of the new creation, is a
further stage in the continuing Fall. Urizen is utterly
impoverished by the separation of Los: Los's acquisi-
tion of a separate selfhood hurts. But Los has work
to do. He may be Apollo, but he has the tools and
methods of Vulcan. Blake must have watched the
work of the smith and the smelter very carefully.

Already in the third 'Memorable Fancy' in *The Marriage of Heaven and Hell* the precious metals of the mind are melted 'into living fluids', and *The Tyger* is the work of an immortal smith. Furnace, anvil, hammer, tongs, chain, bellows—all the means necessary for making harsh material tractable and giving it new (and finite) form—will meet us again and again. The Smith's first work is to bind the changes of Urizen. Chaos, separated from Los, no longer has the impressiveness of the primeval abyss: it is a mere horrible matter of 'hurtling bones'—'Disorganiz'd, rent from Eternity'. Los has to organize him, which he does in the form of the human body, skull and spine, heart, eyes, ears, nostrils, stomach and throat and tongue, limbs—seven ages of creation or states of 'dismal woe' like the woes of The Revelation of St. John. The ambivalence of Los's work is now apparent: it gives form to the chaotic and by that very act confines 'The obscure separation alone'. An appalling thing has happened: this immortal has put on mortality.

> The Immortal endur'd his chains,
> Tho' bound in a deadly sleep.
>
> All the myriads of Eternity,
> All the wisdom & joy of life
> Roll like a sea around him,
> Except what his little orbs
> Of sight by degrees unfold.
>
> And now his eternal life
> Like a dream was obliterated.

In a sense Los is Adam (certainly Los will be to Enitharmon as Adam was to Eve), but he is an Adam who came into separate existence already fallen and who himself fashioned the frame and senses by which man is at once organized and limited. 'Body is a portion of Soul discern'd by the five Senses, the chief inlets of Soul in this age', said 'The voice of the Devil' in *The Marriage of Heaven and Hell.* So the creative soul, the eternal smith, has to make a body because that is the best he can do—and a great deal better than chaotic nothing. After the creative act, after virtue has gone out of the artist, there comes a cold, blank period, and then something new and different happens. The fires of Los decay. He pities Urizen, but 'pity divides the soul'. As God divided the light from the darkness and Eve from Adam, so Los was divided: his softer emotions became an emanation from him, 'the first female form now separate', Enitharmon. 'Eternity shudder'd.' Hitherto male and female qualities had been together in one soul: now both are poorer for the division. Moreover, it marks a further stage of separation from Eternity. Just as Los had been commissioned to keep Urizen to his own place, so now the Eternals spread 'strong curtains' (the veil of this phenomenal world, also called 'Science') to hide the two sexes. We are now in the 'night of Enitharmon's joy', the 'deadly black' of the night that enclosed Oothoon before the second of the three *Visions*: but a startling result of this going back to the beginning of things has been to confirm the darkness, not to show the dawn. Enitharmon at once exhibits 'perverse and cruel delight'. Man begets 'his likeness On his own divided image'. After a remarkable embryological passage, in which some of the description of chaos in the first chapter is deliberately repeated, Orc is born. 'No more Los beheld Eternity.'

So Orc, fiery energy, is primarily just youth, the new birth. His first act of energy is to make his way from the womb. The first result of his birth is the shutting off of his father from Eternity. Orc then, whom we have hitherto looked on as some sort of saviour, of however violent a type, is now discovered

H

to be very much of the fallen world: his arrival, in fact, closed, for a time at any rate, the last cranny of communication with the unfallen world. Paradise is lost: paradise regained can as yet be nothing but the wild and baseless prophecy of *Asia*.

Los has grown tame and melancholy. The red, hunched, howling figure newly wrenched from Urizen had arisen and wrestled with the 'stony sleep' of Urizen. With his mighty hammer he worked at the binding of his changes. Then he wearied and a soft sentimentalism took the place of vigorous work. Now we see him standing, brown-bearded, leaning on his idle hammer while a chain grows round his waist. He looks down on young Orc clinging to his mother. It is a sort of reverse Oedipus-complex, a Laius-complex: the older generation is jealous of the younger: Abraham will sacrifice Isaac. Orc is bound to a rock with 'the Chain of Jealousy Beneath Urizen's deathful shadow'. So the man and woman looking at the chained Orc above the Preludium to *America* were his parents. Aged ignorance is not without malice, but 'how Enitharmon wept' at this Urizenic education.

Nevertheless, at 'the voice of the child' dead things awoke to life, including Urizen. The stream of newly arriving lives keeps the world going and Urizen enters on a new phase. Separated as he is not only from eternity but from poetry, love, and imaginative energy, he awakens to what is left for him, his scientific curiosity and his instinct for imposing cosmos on chaos. He sets out with the lantern of intellect to explore. He is at least a more dignified and purposeful old man than the extraordinary short-arm-balancing figure with waving legs who 'self balanc'd, stretch'd o'er the void' in his early struggles with chaos. We are now getting into the world we know. There has been no single 'Let there be light' act of creation: it has been an evolutionary process. Nor has there been a definite

second fall, a 'Man's first disobedience': death and all
our woe come from the original self-withdrawal of an
eternal being: the spiritual world is one.

'Urizen explor'd his dens.' The four elements, with
whose spiritual forms he had fought in Chaos, now have
form in the phenomenal world. They are the creations
of the truncated soul: very powerful and melancholy
is the picture showing them coming into existence.
These are his sons: his daughters, also first known in
Chaos, are the lower forms of animate life. Then, like
Tiriel, he cursed his sons and daughters for he saw that
his iron laws of peace in uniformity could not be kept.
Life lives upon death,

> The Ox in the slaughter house moans,
> The Dog at the wintry door.

In a very strange picture a vast dog lifts up its head and
howls, while a child stands with clasped hands praying
to an unhearing deity. Over the sorrows of the world
Urizen sorrows, but he cannot change or enlarge what
has become his nature. So, as he moves about spinning
out his cold sorrows like a spider's threads, they
eventually form an all-entangling web—'the Net of
Religion'. It is a hypocrisy that proceeds, so to speak,
from Urizen's very entrails. The realities of eternal
life are quite forgotten: 'laws of prudence' are called
'laws of God'. All this happened in Africa, then called
Egypt. The book ends with the Exodus, viewed as a
flight from Urizen under the leadership of Fuzon
(Fire), the Burning Bush and the Pillar of Fire. Urizen
is left, as the last picture shows, enmeshed in his own
web of religion. *The Book of Urizen* is a history of
developing evil, of the growth of the religion of the
'primeval Priest' against which Blake was in full
rebellion. The symbol of the net or web goes back to
Poetical Sketches ('his silken net') and, in its reference

to religion, to *The Marriage of Heaven and Hell*, where
Swedenborg imagined 'himself the single one on earth
that ever broke a net'. It was part of Blake's thought at
this time and he had to bring it in. The method of
doing so, the spider-threads spun by Urizen as he
moved about, may at first appear forced and even
grotesque, but it does, in fact, bear thinking out.
Nevertheless, the process in Blake's mind is worth
noting: it explains how many of the difficulties or
obscurities in him came about. His visions were dis-
crete: though they sprang from a fundamental unity in
his mind, they often cannot be visually harmonized in
terms of this phenomenal world. Yet they were all
parts of one grand unitary Vision or Revelation. He
has to make them coalesce. Even so the biblical writer,
with whom he had perhaps most in common, saw one
who 'had in his right hand seven stars: and out of his
mouth went a sharp two-edged sword', and later 'a
Lamb as it had been slain, having seven horns and
seven eyes . . . opened one of the seals' of a book.

Of the two sequels to *The Book of Urizen*, both dated
1795, *The Book of Los* is an amplification of Los's
dealings with Urizen. The title-page shows a back view
of Los seated and closely imprisoned in rocks. *The
Book of Urizen* had shown a back view of Los standing
and straining with all his limbs against the rocky sides
and roof of his prison. The new poem dwells on the
horror of his imprisonment, on his rending of the rock
(this is the same as the wrenching apart from Urizen,
for Urizen was a 'petrific abominable chaos'), his Fall
and his partial recovery. He then creates phenomenal
light and its focus, the Sun, which, like the newly
created Earth in *Paradise Lost* (VII, 242), stood 'self-
balanc'd'. To this 'glowing illusion' Los bound 'the
vast Spine of Urizen'. This is, in the first place, a
gloss on the biblical 'Let there be light' and, in the
second place, an account of the way in which Urizen

became subject to sun-measured time. He has found
'a solid' but not 'without fluctuation'. At the top of the
first page Urizen is depicted holding the stone tables of
the law and is entirely inside his net, which extends
below his feet to enclose Man and Woman.

The Book of Ahania is much more of a real sequel to
The Book of Urizen: (it is also in a sense a sequel to
Visions of the Daughters of Albion). It has a double
starting-point in *The Book of Urizen*, Fuzon at the end
of that book and a picture, in the middle of it, of a
female figure floating in air, whom we recognize as
Ahania from the title-page of her own book. Its first
two chapters describe a Homeric battle. Fuzon hurled
a comet at Urizen, who defended himself in vain with
a broad shield like Satan's 'Of tenfold Adamant' and
'vast circumference' in *Paradise Lost*. The great beam
of light divided his 'cold loins' and Ahania was separated from him—not Athene from the head, but
Aphrodite from the loins of this Zeus. Milton's Sin
sprang from Satan's head. Urizen recognized Ahania
as Sin, 'Kissing her and weeping over her'. He is the
'primeval Priest'.

> She fell down, a faint shadow wand'ring
> In chaos, and circling dark Urizen
> As the moon, anguish'd, circles the earth,
> Hopeless, abhorr'd, a death-shadow,
> Unseen, unbodied, unknown,
> The mother of Pestilence.

Urizen, whose dire contemplations now created lust-
formed monsters, fashioned from one of them a
mighty bow and with it shot a poisonous rock at Fuzon,
who thought in his folly that mere light was omnipot-
ent. Fuzon the beautiful was struck dead, like Baldur.

> But the rock fell upon the Earth
> Mount Sinai in Arabia.

The quotation from Galatians is even more effective than in its original setting.

Here for the first time Blake makes use of the symbol of the bow. He did not relinquish it. The black bow of this book reappears in *Jerusalem* 52 ('When Satan first the black bow bent'), and there is the tremendous picture of the mounted archer in *Jerusalem* 39, but there are also 'my Bow of burning gold' in the Preface to *Milton*, the bowstring which 'breathes with ardor' in the victorious conclusion of *Jerusalem*, and the 'arrow from the Almighty's bow' in *The Grey Monk*.

The third chapter of *The Book of Ahania* introduces the tree of Mystery, a permanent symbol from this time on. Of this (unlike the bow) Blake's sources— what fired his imagination—are obvious. 'Mystery' comes from Revelation xvii. 5, where, in the Authorized Version, it is printed in capital letters and followed, also in capitals, by 'Babylon the Great, the mother of harlots and abominations of the earth'. In the Greek the word 'mystery' was presumably a mere parenthetical signpost meaning 'by Babylon understand something else which it is not wise to state plainly', i.e. Rome: but the capitals were too much for Blake, especially as he did think that the Church went in for a great deal of mystification and hocus pocus. The tree comes from *Paradise Lost*, IX, 1101–10, where the tree from which Adam and Eve took fig leaves 'broad as Amazonian Targe' is described. It is the banyan which—

In Malabar or Decan spreds her Armes
Braunching so broad and long, that in the ground
The bended Twigs take root, a Pillard shade
High overarch't, and echoing Walks between.

Urizen, having killed Fuzon, sat on a rock.

Soon shot the pained root
Of Mystery under his heel:
It grew a thick tree: he wrote
In silence his book of iron,
Till the horrid plant, bending its boughs,
Grew to roots when it felt the earth,
And again sprung to many a tree.

This thick-growing, self-rooting vegetation was all the more symbolical of the world of the mere senses because it was from it that Adam and Eve took those leaves which indecently emphasized what they hid. To this tree 'Urizen nail'd Fuzon's corse'. Round it 'flew the arrows of pestilence'. It is the forty years' wandering in the wilderness. We are there still. To Sinai and to that have come the hopes of the Exodus.

The last chapter contains the lament of Ahania. No Song of Solomon now. Far away are 'the bliss of eternal valleys' and the 'golden palace'. There has been a further division. Urizen separated from his emanation is more unhealthy than ever, and his emanation weeps incessantly. So did Oothoon wail 'every morning'.

The Book of Los and *The Book of Ahania* are engraved in the ordinary, not Blake's usual reversed, way. They are only slightly illustrated. This seems a further indication of the petering out of the Lambeth books, of which they and *The Song of Los* are the last. Yet in pictorial inspiration 1795 was a magnificent year, the year of the great colour-prints. The moments of vision were as frequent and fruitful as at any time: to synthesize them in words was another matter.

Blake's rebellion against the ordinary conception of the world and the consequences of that conception, whether in religion, morals, politics, or art, was strong and consistent. The urge to get to something more positive than rebellion was also strong and consistent. The positive was implicit in the negative, and at times became explicit, but a continuance of 'the Bible of Hell' did not seem the right road. There was an interval, and then Blake made a new beginning.

CHAPTER V

THE PROPHET

The Four Zoas

BLAKE produced so much in 1795 and must have been so busy in 1796 and the early part of 1797 on the 537 designs for Young's *Night Thoughts* that he can hardly have begun *The Four Zoas* before 1797. It was not published: the MS.[1] is in the British Museum. Two-thirds of it is written on proof sheets of the engravings for *Night Thoughts*. He first called it *Vala*, the title-page in its original form reading 'VALA / or / The Death and / Judgement / of the Eternal Man / A DREAM / of Nine Nights / by William Blake 1797'. The date, on the analogy of *Milton* and *Jerusalem*, may only indicate the year when the poem was begun, but it may safely be assumed that he had written at least seven Nights before going to Felpham in September 1800. He took the MS. with him to Felpham, and there, in the light of developing ideas and new visions, he made extensive additions and alterations. At a second revision less extensive changes were made in pencil. But it would not do. He gave it up, and started afresh first with *Milton* and then with *Jerusalem*, in both of which he incorporated some passages from the abandoned *The Four Zoas*.

The fiction of a dream is not maintained and disappears from the revised title-page. The 'Nine Nights' (the nine books continued to be called 'Night the First', &c.) are an imitation of the nine nights of Young's *Night Thoughts*, a strong indication that he

---

[1] Evidently begun as a fair copy, which explains why some of it is now palimpsest over deletion.

began *Vala* after his work on that book. Vala (to be pronounced not Vahla or Valla but Veila) is the Veil of the phenomenal world, of Nature, the 'strong curtains' of *The Book of Urizen*. The 'Four Zoas', after whom Blake finally decided to call the poem, are the 'Four Mighty Ones . . . in every Man', the four active principles in the soul. They seem to correspond to the 'four beasts' or 'living creatures' (Zoa) of The Revelation of St. John. At Felpham he learnt Greek: 'I go on Merrily with my Greek and Latin. . . . I read Greek as fluently as an Oxford scholar & the Testament is my chief master: astonishing indeed is the English Translation, it is almost word for word', he wrote on 30 January 1803 to his brother James. At about this time he must have changed the title of his poem. An Oxford scholar could have told him that Zoa was the plural of Zoön, but we might have lost the nice Blakean uniqueness of the double plural, 'Zoas'.

In *The Book of Urizen* the Fall and Creation were explained as a series of disruptions following the self-withdrawal of Urizen. In *The Four Zoas* also there is a 'fall into Division' which is to end in a 'Resurrection to Unity'. The Zoas (Urizen, Los, Luvah, Tharmas) are divided among themselves and each is divided from his counterpart (Ahania, Enitharmon, Vala, Enion). Otherwise there are many differences from the Lambeth books. It is a new attempt at a psychologico-cosmic myth, at spiritual history.

Some passages of the poem in its first form were erased and additions written over the erasures: perhaps modern photography could recover them. If so, the original poem could then be printed for the first time. Meanwhile, it can, except for erased passages, be laboriously disentangled from the Oxford edition (1926) of the Prophetic Books by anyone who carefully studies the textual notes. The Nonesuch edition isolates the penultimate version by italicizing the pencil additions.

Of the pictures three are reproduced in the Oxford edition, four in Wright's *Life of William Blake*, one in Plowman's *Introduction to the Study of Blake* and one in Keynes's *Pencil Drawings*. Nineteen pages were reproduced, more or less, in smaller facsimile by Ellis and Yeats in 1893. The lack of even such an imperfect printed text as is possible of the original *Vala* without additions is a real handicap to the study of Blake's development. It is as if we had neither Keats's *Hyperion* nor *The Fall of Hyperion* (also 'a dream') but a MS. of the first changed by addition, deletion, and erasure into a semblance of the second with some further pencilled afterthoughts: we should not be satisfied with a printed version of the final hotch-potch as it was, very properly, abandoned by its author.

It was abandoned by Blake because the new wine was bursting the old bottles. He poured it into the new bottles of *Milton* and *Jerusalem* where we shall study it. Here we shall confine ourselves for the moment to the old wine—the original *Vala* as far as it can be disentangled. It opens with the separation of Tharmas from his affective part, Enion. Tharmas-Enion is the instinctive unitary life, the life of Innocence, the life which Wordsworth, looking back on his boyhood, saw he had then so largely lived. His 'Recollections of Early Childhood' gave him *Intimations of Immortality*, but the gleam was lost in experience, as that *Ode* and *The Prelude* and *Lines on an Evening of Extraordinary Splendour* show. Tharmas cries—

Lost! Lost! Lost! are my Emanations! Enion! come forth. We are become a Victim to the Living. We hide in Secret.

Enion, while united with Tharmas, is the 'Joy' of Coleridge's *Dejection*, but after the separation—

I see, not feel, how beautiful they are.

For Wordsworth, in the *Ode to Duty*, 'joy' is no longer 'its own security', impulse must give place to law. So Enion finds 'stern demands of Right & Duty instead of Liberty'. Tharmas, the 'Parent power', the innocence who in one sense is the child-father of the man, has to make room in himself for new experience which he cannot refuse. Every new experience modifies the experiencer: he has to adapt himself or to refuse to adapt himself. The old self is 'jealous' of the new: it is full of 'fear'. It may attempt to withdraw into itself, to 'hide in Secret'. Unable to combine adaptability with integrity, it falls 'into Division'. Tharmas goes underground, or rather underwater, and Enion will eventually disappear leaving only a wailing voice, a deepseated sorrow for lost paradise.

The instinctive life is not, however, simply banished from consciousness. Separated from 'Eternity' it appears to fallen man as mere physical life, as Tharmas's Spectre. The use of this word, with which from now on we shall be familiar, is typical of Blake's genius. The 'spectres of the dead' are not their souls, but their unreal unsouled physical appearances: yet they are the shadows, distorted into a semblance of solidity, of something real. The Spectre of Tharmas is formidable, cruel, self-righteous, Theotormon and Bromion in one. The separated Enion is afraid and horribly attracted. They unite in 'a bright wonder, Nature, Half Woman & half Spectre' and Enion brings forth 'two little Infants', Los and Enitharmon, who abandon her as soon as they need no longer 'sulk upon her breast'. Enion fades; for they are savage children.

This is quite a different origin for Los and Enitharmon from that given in *The Book of Urizen*. Enitharmon is here no Eve produced from Los.

Nine Times they liv'd among the forest feeding on sweet fruits;

And nine bright Spaces wander'd, weaving mazes of
   delight,
Snaring the wild Goats for their milk; they eat the flesh
   of Lambs,
A male & female, naked & ruddy as the pride of summer.

Alternate Love & Hate his breast, hers Scorn & Jealousy
In embryon passions: they kiss'd not, nor embrac'd, for
   shame & fear.
His head beam'd light, & in his vigorous voice was
   prophecy.
He could controll the times & seasons & the days &
   years:
She could controll the spaces, regions, desert, flood &
   forest.
They wander'd long, till they sat down upon the margin'd sea
Conversing with the visions of Beulah in dark slumber-
   ous bliss.

The Los-Enitharmon activity of the soul emerges,
so to speak, from the disintegration of primal innocence. It has within it the potentiality of redemption
by reintegration, but at first it is crude. The men and
women in whom it is found live in the state of love-and-
hate which produced them, and their poetic creation is
concerned with the phenomenal-noümenal world of
Time and Space. Los and Enitharmon, the inspira-
tional and affective parts of the one activity, are not
now separated to the extent that Tharmas and Enion
are separated, but they are represented as aggressive
and quarrelsome youth 'Craving the more, the more
enjoying'. Their Nuptial Feast is 'the Feast of envy',
and the 'Nuptial Song' of strife and confusion is
followed by the voice of Enion lamenting the cruelty
of animal life: the aggregate of emotion in instinctive
Nature is one of helpless sorrow.
   Meanwhile we have been reintroduced to Urizen

and introduced to the remaining Zoa, Luvah. It must be remembered that there is nothing fixed or final about any of the Zoas or their feminine counterparts. They are not persons but recurrent elements of the soul which change their character and activity according to the action of other elements and the degree of their 'fall'. Urizen and Luvah (Orc will eventually turn out to be Luvah) are closely combined in this book's version of their fall. Intellectual energy and emotional energy, head and heart, each has his proper station in 'eternity', but 'Urizen sleeps in the porch' and Luvah flies 'up from the Human Heart Into the Brain'. Like Phaethon, about whom Blake read in Ovid, 'Luvah siez'd the Horses of Light & rose into the Chariot of Day'. Phaethon's prank was disastrous for himself and the earth: so was Luvah's for himself and the whole 'Eternal Man'. As a result of Intellect sleeping and Emotion taking his place Emotion in his 'original glory' is lost. Instead we have only Luvah's feminine counterpart, Vala, the beauty of this world and all the feelings which that evokes. The emotional world is in chaos: there will be terrible wars. To guard against that Urizen is summoned: after softheadedness comes hardheartedness. Urizen declares, 'I am God from Eternity to Eternity' (so had the mistaken Fuzon cried, 'I am God, eldest of things'). At the request of fallen man, Urizen builds a material, mathematic world. This gives the fallen man and, in him, Urizen a chance of keeping off Luvah—fallen Luvah of whom they are afraid—though it brings Urizen no freedom from misgivings and has many evil consequences. Rationalism and planning are evils used to fight the evils of chaotic emotion.

Los and Enitharmon live happily in this developed world, but their 'golden heavens tremble' when 'from the dark deep' is heard the wail from Enion. This great lyric begins:

I am made to sow the thistle for wheat, the nettle for a
    nourishing dainty:
I have planted a false oath in the earth; it has brought
    forth a poison tree:
I have chosen the serpent for a councellor, & the dog
For a schoolmaster to my children.

Enion's lament is heard by Ahania: Emanation calls
to Emanation. This leads to a new version of the
separation of Ahania from Urizen. Ahania, the affective element in Urizen, his emanation or feminine
counterpart, is externalized as Woman the plaything.
Woman the plaything, touched with pity at Enion's
lament, at the hidden sorrowfulness of fallen life, has
a glimpse of the Divine Vision (Night III, 35–7).

       these dens thy wisdom fram'd,
Golden & beautiful, but O how unlike those sweet fields
    of bliss
Where liberty was justice, & eternal science was mercy!

She tells Urizen (lines 44–60) what a false god he is
to man and how a surprising visitation of passion
(Luvah) follows man's worship of the false god and how
there then comes a separation of passion from its
feminine counterpart (Vala). In fact, once Intellect
and Passion have left their proper stations and balance
of functions, there is a vicious alternation of Luvah-
Urizen-Luvah and so on recurring. On hearing
Ahania's reproach Urizen casts her out and at once
falls himself. No Zoa can maintain itself without its
counterpart.
    From the ruin of the reign of 'reason' there emerges
in conflict and misery the instinctive life, but Tharmas
and Enion cannot unite and Enion is lost again. The
materialist world and its god have gone down because
of a feminine sensibility. No positive good has so far
resulted. Redemption is not in sight.

Tharmas (who, minus Enion, is mere primal life bereft of joy) succeeds as God. First Luvah reigned for a short time, then Urizen, now Tharmas—Los's pretensions get him nowhere. Tharmas, after giving the recalcitrant Los a taste of his power, orders him to bind Urizen to prevent his restoration as king. He is to rebuild the furnaces, the spiritual activities which have gone out with the ruin of intellect: the Poetic Genius is now given a chance with Enitharmon, wayward woman ultimately a partner, as reward. There follows an account of the binding of Urizen not much different from that in *The Book of Urizen* and ending with the same weakening of Los.

> Terrified at the shapes
> Enslav'd humanity put on, he became what he beheld.

Los's terrific activities have a frightening and taming effect on Enitharmon.

Los is not God, but he is the vice-regent for Tharmas. Intellect and Passion have made a mess of it: Inspiration has gone back to dependence on Instinct.

It is far from being a complete success. At the beginning of Night v—

> Infected, Mad, he danc'd on his mountains high & dark as heaven.
> Now fix'd into one stedfast bulk, his features Stonify.

It is an Ovidian metamorphosis and may well hint at Stonehenge and Avebury as perverted productions of Inspiration. The deterioration of the Poetic Genius and of its counterpart in the feminine affections leads to the birth of 'a terrible Child', revolutionary energy, which the Poetic Genius, in jealousy and self-defensive fears, chains to earth against the wish of the feminine affections. We are back on familiar ground. When, too late, Los tries to unchain Orc, the chains have grown into the rock. Enitharmon in her grief has a revelation of the repressed energies of Vala, Ahania, Orc, and Urizen and hears Urizen's long lament on his great mistake, exchanging with Luvah his horses for Luvah's wine, and his determination to 'explore these dens', i.e. to try to understand underlying spiritual causes and events.

In Night VI Urizen's daughters (habits, rather than systems, of thought) first stop him and then give way. He curses them. He withstands a temptation to end the life of both mind and body and investigates and records a dark underworld of the mind, but he never reaches the finality at which he aims. He falls back on the web or net of religion.

In Night VII as first written (VIIa in the Oxford text, VIIb in the Nonesuch) and arranged (i.e. beginning at the present line 121, 'Now in the Caverns') we have arrived at the same point as the Preludium to *America*, the mating of Orc with the natural world. There it was a prelude of faith and hope, here it is the ruin of both. The 'shadowy female' is rent 'into a formless indefinite' and strewn 'on the Abyss' (i.e. of the five senses, cf. *The Marriage of Heaven and Hell*), and Orc becomes the serpent wreathed round the tree of Mystery. Perverted he is now a destructive ally of Urizen: this may be understood on the sexual or political or religious plane. Moreover Vala (still pining for Luvah) keeps Tharmas (still pining for Enion) under control. Urizen envisages complete triumph with commerce, black religion, and war. Tharmas and Los serve him: Enitharmon is afraid but ignorant. The Prester Serpent, minister of the perverted Church, is shown in both words and picture.

At this point something happened to Blake. It shook him. A later passage beginning 'Then I heard the Earthquake', of which only those five words survive, was intended as an addition to Night VII. He

I

tried changing round the first and second halves of that Night. It would not do: he set about writing a new and different Night VII.

Near the end of Night VI Urizen's investigations brought him nearer and nearer to Orc (passionate energy, including that of sex) who is chained in his underworld. He was stopped temporarily by a Freudian censor or rather double censor, Tharmas and the Spectre of Urthona. Tharmas as instinct we know. Who or what is Urthona? Whatever Blake may have meant by him in earlier years, he is now one whose symbol is hammer and anvil: he is a smith, a Maker. As one of the ultimate spiritual elements he is, therefore, the creative (that is the imaginative) element. 'On earth', i.e. in the fallen, phenomenal world, he is represented by Los. The 'Spectre of Urthona', the unreal, framework appearance of the real Creator, must be the distorted and skeletonized idea of the Maker of the world which the average man calls 'God': it is the dry bones of religion, Superstition. Yet even such an idea of God will give the investigating intellect pause, for the Spectre of Urthona still represents creation and Urizen's search will end, as we shall see in Night VII, in uncreation—in freeing Orc only to reduce him to a serpent wreathed round a tree and his potencies to forbidden fruit shining sinfully.

If Man is made in the image of God, God must display the image of Man. In so far as Man can be called Divine, God can be called Human. Man's business is to strive to become entirely Human. The creative element in him, Los the Maker, is identical with the creative element in God, the name of which 'in eternity' is Urthona. The Los in Blake had hitherto rejected the current inadequate presentations of Urthona, the 'Spectre of Urthona'. Blake had been a rebel against God and Christianity. Now by a sudden illumination, which shook him like an earthquake, he

recognized that Los and the Spectre of Urthona were
brothers, derived from the one Urthona.

> Los Embrac'd the Spectre, first as a brother,
> Then as another Self, astonish'd, humanizing & in tears,
> In Self abasement Giving up his Domineering lust.
> (VII, lines 335–7)

(The last two words have caused unnecessary difficulty.
They mean 'lust for domineering', the 'dark self-
righteous pride' of the poem in *Jerusalem* 27.)

What led up to this is of great interest. First, Urizen
retires[1] into his Web and thereby turns Superstition
into a herald and ally, then brushes aside the double
censor, Tharmas and the Spectre, and finds Orc
chained. 'Brooding Envious over Orc' he sits for ages
while the banyan tree of Mystery grows round him as
in *The Book of Ahania*. Orc, in a 'burning clime' of
self-produced fires which certainly include the fires of
sex, has 'feet & hands . . . nail'd to the burning rock',
but prefers that to the unchained horror of icy Urizen.
Yet Urizen's 'Cold hypocrisy' wins. Not 'the shadowy
female', as in the first form of Night VII, but Urizen
by his hypocrisy tames Orc into a serpent climbing his
tree of Mystery. Beneath it are Los and Enitharmon
whom we last saw in Night V after their unavailing
attempt to unchain Orc. In the passage which follows
(lines 166–331) the cosmic and the autobiographic are
inextricably mixed. Los alternates with the Spectre
(who is his other self), Enitharmon with the Shadow of
Enitharmon (who is her mortal and limited self).
They tell one another a new and complementary
version of the Fall of Man, who was seduced by the
gentle passions, Vala. Urizen was born of that union,
and then Vala was divided into Vala and Luvah,
feminine and masculine love. Urizen grew up and then

---

[1] The Spectre straddles the vale like Bunyan's Apollyon,
but Urizen does not fight.

there was a conspiracy between Urizen and Luvah against the Man. So might run the course of any spiritual history after a perfectly genuine love match. So, perhaps they decided, it had been with William and Catherine: but now Enitharmon, who had once brought forth Orc, brings forth Vala. Whatever may be meant by this in Catherine's emotional history, 'the Gates of Enitharmon's heart' could never be closed again, and, though it was something on the natural plane, this experience of Enitharmon immediately preceded Los's conversion.

> But then the Spectre enter'd Los's bosom. Every sigh
>   & groan
> Of Enitharmon bore Urthona's Spectre on its wings.
> Obdurate Los felt Pity. Enitharmon told the tale
> Of Urthona. Los Embrac'd the Spectre. . . .

One is so used to thinking of Catherine as an example of Shakespeare's 'So wears she to him' that it is exciting to find Catherine responsible for William's conversion.

It happened late in 1799 or early in 1800. The letter to Cumberland of 23 December 1796 with its mention of 'Nature & Providence, the Eternal Parents' indicates quite a different frame of mind. The three letters of August 1799 do not suggest the conversion. The next two letters, those to Hayley on 1 April and 6 May 1800 ('Jesus and his Angels' . . . 'my enthusiasm which I wish all to partake of . . . By it I am the companion of angels'), and, of course, the letter to Butts of 2 October 1800 ('I am the determined advocate of Religion & Humility'), do show the change. The move to Felpham, the new start, was caused by this earthquake of an imaginative experience, Blake's new acceptance of Christianity—an acceptance which was caused, accompanied, and followed by a renewal at a deeper level of his and Catherine's conjugal life. The Christianity, of course, would be non-Urizenic, which would be one reason why some should say it was not Christianity. Yet even for Urizen, being one of the 'Four Mighty Ones', he must feel 'love & not hate', though this was not recorded until a later revision (VII, 492). Meanwhile a universal process was exemplified when William and Catherine came to a fuller understanding of themselves and of each other and of their place in the scheme of things. They worked together, reconciled at the deepest level. Within themselves they could see 'the Lamb of God . . . descending to redeem', and in Night VIII Blake, for the first time in his poetry, is primarily concerned with the Crucifixion.

This is the point at which the rebel became the prophet. The change, as applied to Enitharmon, is well illustrated by two pictures (Wright I, 161). The first, at the bottom of p. 6 of the later Night VII, shows Enitharmon turning the starry wheel, the night sky. The second, at the bottom of p. 6 of Night VIII, shows her pushing it away. In the first she is the feminine principle of Nature, the mere 'love that makes the world go round' and never get anywhere. In the second she is no longer content to be the slave-mistress of a 'Circle of Destiny': she pushes away this dark appearance which is mostly voids between the stars. The lines immediately above this picture are—

He stood in fair Jerusalem to awake up into Eden
The fallen Man; but first to Give his vegetated body
To be cut off & separated, that the Spiritual body may
    be Reveal'd.

The conversion was a double one, of man and wife. The divine vision was a vision of the divine and of themselves in it. From the simple Christianity of the Lamb in *Songs of Innocence* and from the insight of

To Tirzah Blake had for a time fallen away. He saw his error. He experienced a 'last judgment'. He had been wrong in attacking religion as such. Henceforth, and especially in *Jerusalem*, his attack is on perverted religion, on Deism masquerading as Christianity.

In Night VIII, omitting later additions, we have, as we might expect, the first sign of life in the sleeping, i.e. fallen, man. Like the Shunammite's son he sneezed seven times. Los and Enitharmon behold the Divine Vision and carry on their joint work of artistic creation. The Lamb (lines 54–7) is seen in Luvah's robes, i.e. Jesus is seen to be love. The suppressed love who is Orc results in wars for which Urizen provides the weapons. Los and Enitharmon work against them. Vala (the 'Shadowy Female', the Enitharmon of *Europe*), feminine love, laments for Luvah. This is the normal, but visionless, human longing for a world of peace and love. It leads to 'sorrow, lust, repentance' (line 174). She is against the Lamb whom she considers Luvah's murderer (for the Divine Vision leaves mere mortal passion far behind). The artistic creations of Los and Enitharmon go on. These creations are Jerusalem, a veil within which the Lamb may be seen (line 184). After a song of the Sons of Eden Satan and the Lamb face one another (line 258). With Satan are Tirzah and her sisters tormenting and restricting the 'poor human form'. The Lamb is condemned and crucified on the tree of Mystery.

Darkness & sorrow cover'd all flesh. Eternity was darken'd.

(line 403)

The symbolic significance of the Crucifixion is clear. Now (lines 401–54) Urizen, in the form of the Dantesque or Miltonic Satan (Lucifer prone), repines at the ascendancy of Orc. A stony stupor overcomes Urizen and Tharmas and Urthona and Los, but

Tharmas and Urthona give their power to Los. There is a despairing lament of Ahania answered by Enion's song of coming redemption.

And Los & Enitharmon took the Body of the Lamb
Down from the Cross, & plac'd it in a Sepulcher which
    Los had hewn
For himself in the Rock of Eternity: trembling & in
    despair
Jerusalem wept over the Sepulcher two thousand Years.

In Night IX (lines 1–89 are a later addition) Man on his Rock calls on Urizen in 'his scaly form' to resume but not exceed his proper functions. Urizen recognizes his previous error. Then (line 229) 'the bursting Universe explodes'. It is the Last Judgement. Tyranny is destroyed, for the Last Judgement means the recognition and thereby the destruction of error.

And the Fall'n Man, who was arisen upon the Rock of
    Ages,
Beheld the Vision of God; & he arose up from the Rock.
And Urizen arose up with him, walking thro' the
    flames
To meet the Lord coming to Judgment; but the flames
    repell'd them
Still to the Rock: in vain they strove to Enter the
    Consummation
Together; for the Redeem'd Man could not enter the
    Consummation.

So (lines 290–341) Urizen and his sons (systems of thought) plough, sow with souls and harrow the earth, getting rid of weeds and turning weapons into useful tools. They wait for the harvest, Orc being now the ripening sun. This does not mean actual political and social reorganization under enlightened Reason but Reason at work upon existing political and social organization. Next (lines 342–83) Ahania revives.

Orc ceases to be Orc and becomes Luvah again. Luvah and Vala resume their proper functions, i.e. mutual human love resumes its innocence and no longer tries to dominate brain or heart.

Lines 384–556 form the Arcadian interlude of Luvah and Vala in 'lower Paradise'. Tharmas and Enion are rediscovered as children 'in Vala's world'. Nature is sweet and simple to the young in happy love.

Meanwhile the human harvest is ready and is reaped by Urizen and his sons. Enion and Tharmas join the harvest feast at which the Eternal Man sits. But Man is still man (and woman) and incapable of sustained reality. Men are shadows of the Eternals and are watched over by them. After the harvest is the threshing and winnowing: there is an end to 'Mystery'. After that the vintage is ready and the grapes are trodden in the winepress of Luvah: from all the pain of passion is made the Human Wine. Next Urthona-Los grinds the corn, the storms of Tharmas turning the windmills. Urthona builds ovens and bakes the bread—'the bread of knowledge' (line 818), 'the Bread of Ages' (line 820). At last, after all this, man is what he is meant to be.

The Last Judgement (the rejection of error and revelation of truth) is, it should be noted, a beginning not an end. After it the sacramental Bread and Wine must be made for man to live on. Their making is painful. They are the sublimated work of Reason and Passion.

On the Sunday before he set out for Felpham in September 1800 Blake wrote to Mrs. Flaxman in joyful anticipation: Felpham would be his Bethel.

You stand in the village & look up to heaven;
The precious stones glitter on flights seventy-seven;
And My Brother is there, & My Friend & Thine
Descend & ascend with the Bread & the Wine.

The Bread of sweet Thought & the Wine of Delight
Feeds the Village of Felpham by day & by night;
And at his own door the bless'd Hermit does stand,
Dispensing, Unceasing, to all the whole Land.

Robert would be there and would be intimately concerned with *Milton*. There would be much Bread and Wine, some of it bitter: and Hermit Hayley would turn out to be a corporeal friend but a spiritual enemy, not one of the angels ascending and descending the ladder between earth and heaven.

If the reader will bracket off in the Oxford edition the passages stated in the notes to be additions and will take the summary given above as a guide, he should get a fair idea of the nature and purpose of the original poem, Man's 'fall into Division & his Resurrection to Unity'. It would be rash to assume that every correction and addition was made as part of a general revision, but the most important of them certainly were. It was in the course of writing the poem that Blake had his revelation. Los and Enitharmon settle down to create Jerusalem or to build the city of Art whose odd name Golgonooza suggests that it is derived from New Golgotha. So, though he also made additions to the latest Nights, he had more especially to go back to the earlier ones and try to bring them into line with his new ideas. In the process of revision still fresh ideas occurred and demanded expression. New passages were written which break the old sequence of both story and thought and make the poem much more difficult to read, e.g. Night VIII, lines 330–402, in which Rahab, the perverted Church, is introduced and is instructed, unavailingly, by Los in the doctrine of States and the history of religions.

The MS. contains five full-page pictures, but Blake's general plan was to leave blank about a quarter of each page at the bottom for a picture which could, if he

wished, be continued in the wide margin at the side of
the text. He was simply imitating his own method with
Young's *Night Thoughts* where the text is in the middle
of the pages and the picture below, at the sides and,
sometimes, also above. On one page of *Vala* the picture
interrupts the text and may have been drawn then and
there.

Milton

The more Blake patched with new cloth the old
garment of Nights I to VI the more obvious the rent.
Moreover he was getting some still newer cloth and
patching Nights VII to IX with that. It would not do.
He started afresh with a new poem, *Milton*, but the
Felpham years during which he had graduated from
Vala to *Milton* had immensely deepened his insight and
had made its expression in 'a selection of language
really used by men' more and more impossible. There
had been moments of illumination and there had been
continuous 'Mental Fight'. So, whereas most of the
original *Vala* described psychological happenings in
language of at least comparative simplicity and surface
intelligibility, we get henceforth more and more of
the product of Blake's mind coming out in a densely
compact form. Contrast *The Four Zoas*, I, 19, 20—

Lost! Lost! Lost! are my Emanations! Enion! come
    forth.
We are become a Victim to the Living. We hide in
    Secret.

with *Milton*, 3^{26}–4^1 (2^{26}–3^1, Keynes)

Three Classes are Created by the Hammer of Los, &
    Woven
From Golgonooza, the spiritual Four-fold London
    eternal.

The first passage can be explained in a few sentences, the second needs a knowledge of all Blake.

Of the four existing copies of *Milton* none, as the paper shows, can have been printed earlier than 1808 and one is on paper watermarked 1815. An internal reference to 'Hand' (the accusing hand of Hunt of *The Examiner*) also shows that the date 1804 on the title-page cannot be that of completion, though the title-page may have been engraved in that year. It shows Milton with right foot and right hand forward advancing into a column of fire 'To justify the Ways of God to Men'. Milton, we remember, exalted light above heat and did not enter the flames of his own hell. In *Milton* Blake's favourite poet will repair his errors. For 'Corporeal War', such as that in Heaven on which Milton, 'curb'd by the general malady & infection from the silly Greek & Latin slaves of the Sword', had spent so much time in *Paradise Lost*, the *Preface* calls on 'Young Men of the New Age' to substitute 'Mental War'. All that is needed is to be

just & true to our own Imaginations, those Worlds of Eternity in which we shall live for ever in Jesus our Lord.

And did those feet in ancient time
Walk upon England's mountains green?

Book the First opens with an invocation suggested by Milton's 'Sing, Heavenly Muse'. Throughout this poem autobiography and Blake's deepest imaginative philosophy are found together. Here, at the very beginning, we learn that Milton left heaven 'to go into the deep' to redeem his 'Emanation', all that was dear to him. So Blake left Felpham. The reason for both decisions was the same. It is given in a 'Bard's prophetic Song', which at one level tells the psychological happenings between Blake and Hayley and at another the truth about Satan. Both Blake and Milton must be occupied with the building of 'Jerusalem', whose place in 'The Island white' is now usurped by 'stony Druid Temples'. This marks another new development in Blake's background symbolism. Plate 4 of *Milton* (reproduced in the Oxford edition and in *English Blake*) contains a magnificent example. First we notice a huge trilithon, compared to which those of Stonehenge are a child's toys, a rocking-stone, stars and a waning moon. Under the trilithon runs a road on which a horseman rides sedately but like one in his own country. The figures of horse and rider are very small and details are not easy to make out. Can it be that he is Hayley with or without the umbrella? After all, Blake had a sense of humour. Finally at the bottom, trudging along with staff and pack, is a pilgrim whose home is not here.

Blake's deep interest in druidism, though there is a reference to Avebury in *Europe* 117, may not be earlier than his residence in South Molton Street, but the subject had been much in the air in the eighteenth century and Blake, of course, knew also Milton's suggestion in *Areopagitica* that 'the school of Pythagoras and the Persian wisdom took beginning from the old Philosophy of this Iland'. The eighteenth-century archaeologists argued that *The Patriarchal and Druidical Religion* (the first part of the title of a book by W. Cooke, 1754) was the same. Stukeley (1687–1765) is the best-known exponent of the theory. It was obvious from the Bible that the original, pure religion was that of the patriarchs—Adam, Noah, Abraham. The earliest inhabitants of Britain, as of other countries, could have had no other religion. So the mysterious religion of the Druids, known to Caesar and other ancient writers, was that of the patriarchs. 'The patriarchal religion and the Christian is but one and the same' (Stukeley, *Abury*, 1743). So Blake

(*Descriptive Catalogue*, 1809, p. 44), 'All had originally . . . one religion, this was the religion of Jesus, the everlasting Gospel' (Revelation xiv. 6, and notice once more Blake's difficult 'of'—here it is the religion preached by, not about, Jesus). The Druids were the Bishops of the primitive religion. Stukeley wrote on *Balaam Druid*—'Adam was a Druid, and Noah' (Blake, *Descriptive Catalogue*, p. 41). Even with further development, when different nations had different deities, the differences were only on the surface. It was the same deities who were known to different nations by different names, and Bryant's *Analysis of Ancient Mythology* (1774–6), well-known to Blake, was an attempt to make clear the correspondences. *All Religions are One* (and derived from the Poetic Genius) was precisely the subject of one of Blake's early tractates, the other being *There is no Natural Religion*.

Why then did Blake in *Milton* and *Jerusalem* use 'Druidism' and its megalithic remains as a symbol of all that was wrong with religion and mental attitude? The fact that he was already committed to stone, the tables of the Sinaitic law, as a symbol of oppression may have had something to do with it, but the chief reason was human sacrifice. The antiquarians glossed over or excused it, but to Blake it was proof that something had gone terribly wrong with 'the Druidical age, which began to turn allegoric and mental signification into corporeal command, whereby human sacrifice would have depopulated the earth' (*Descriptive Catalogue*, p. 41). The long poem in *Jerusalem* 27 contains Blake's theory. Here in England, where once 'Jerusalem' walked (Albion's 'emanation', the sum and expression of that eternal Man's affections, spiritual religion and converse with God such as the patriarchs had), the 'Druids' golden knife', intended only, as Pliny relates, for the cutting of mistletoe,

Rioted in human gore,
In Offerings of Human Life.

They groan'd aloud on London Stone,
They groan'd aloud on Tyburn's Brook;
Albion gave his deadly groan,
And all the Atlantic Mountains shook.

Albion's Spectre from his Loins,
Tore forth in all the pomp of War;
Satan his name; in flames of fire
He stretch'd his Druid pillars far.

London Stone was supposed to be an altar. The judicial executions at Tyburn were a form of human sacrifice (Blake foreshadowed modern anthropologists as well as modern psychologists). This terrible perversion of religion led to the 'pomp of war' which has since raged over the world.

We do not now build, in the physical sense, temples like Avebury and Stonehenge, but mentally we are in the same state as those 'Druids'. Blake's lifework is to help forward the substitution of 'Jerusalem', a 'building of human souls', for the 'stony Druid temples'. The Bard's song is about Satan, who is not to be made a Druid sacrifice, to be punished vindictively, retributively or in the interests of some abstract Justice, is not, in fact, to be treated as Milton treated him in *Paradise Lost* but much more in the way recommended by *The Little Vagabond*.

Satan and Palamabron in the Bard's song are Hayley and Blake, i.e. they are those elements in Hayley and Blake respectively which were concerned in their relations with another (to begin with—later other elements such as Rintrah, Wrath, or Michael, the traditional fighter against Satan, come in). These elements are not, however, unique in Hayley and Blake: they are common elements in men, and that is why technical names are used. Satan, as in *Job*, is a tormentor and an accuser and, as in *Paradise Lost*, a tempter, but his special method here is that of 'officious brotherhood'. He insists on exchanging tasks with Palamabron so that each does precisely the work for which he is not fitted: it is a neat satire on Hayley's productions as well as an expression of Blake's exasperation at the miniatures and fan-paintings and listening to Klopstock read aloud from which he suffered. Hayley was so nice about it all that Blake almost felt in the wrong, but in the end there was a scene, an outward one with Satan saying 'I am God alone' and an inward one in Blake to be described only as 'Los in his wrath curs'd heaven & earth'. The Druid power was utterly in the ascendant.

Where Satan, making to himself Laws from his own identity,
Compell'd others to serve him in moral gratitude & submission,
Being call'd God, setting himself above all that is callèd God.

Yet Enitharmon 'form'd a Space for Satan', 'a New Space to protect Satan from punishment', i.e. Blake himself, in so far as the affective side of the Poetic Genius was dominant in him, could forgive him that trespassed against him and, instead of wanting to cast him into a Miltonic hell, would give him elbow-room for redemption.

The psychological study of Satan-Hayley went on. Leutha said Satan's sin was her fault. Leutha is, more or less, Venus. Oothoon in *Visions of the Daughters of Albion* plucked 'the bright Marygold of Leutha's vale'. Elynittria, who is Catherine, will presently bring Leutha 'to Palamabron's bed'. Here Leutha springs from the breast (10^{10})[1] or head (10^{38})[1] of Satan, as Sin

[1] 13 (Keynes).

from Satan in *Paradise Lost* II, 758. Whatever Blake
the psychoanalyst had seen in Hayley he depicted in the
second full-page illustration. There on a plinth stands
—not the dignified façade of a statue which the 'bless'd
Hermit' offered to the world but—a Satan writhing in
the flames of 'Rintrah's fury' and of ungratified desires.
Los, with clasped hands, regards him with intense
interest and concern: Enitharmon, who 'form'd a Space',
has one foot, her left foot, on the plinth, though her hands
and right foot turn away. Hayley was twelve years older
than Blake. Engaged to be married at the age of eighteen,
he had, in fact, married someone else six years later, in
1769. In 1780 he became the father of an illegitimate
son, Thomas Alphonso, who died in 1800, when Blake,
still at Lambeth, engraved for Hayley Flaxman's
portrait of him. Hayley's wife had adopted Thomas
Alphonso in 1780, but in 1786 she went out of her
mind, in 1789 a permanent separation was arranged, in
1800 she died. The widower married again in 1809,
and from this wife he was separated in 1812. Mr. Frye,
in attempting to reconstruct Blake's thoughts, writes
(*Fearful Symmetry*, p. 330), 'Hayley had patronized
Cowper, and Cowper had gone mad. He had patronized Blake, and a good many people were saying that
Blake was mad.' The two Mrs. Hayleys do suggest
that Blake was not alone in finding Hayley impossible
at close quarters. And how had he tried to 'act upon my
wife', as Blake wrote in a later and unpublished epigram? Perhaps only by taking some opportunity of
saying, 'Mrs. Blake, could you not persuade your
husband to pay more regard to his own interests and
yours?'

For Hayley-Satan was a good, kind man. If he had
other, unintegrated elements in him, that applied to
everyone. The schizophrenia of Man, his 'fall into
Division', is precisely Blake's lament. Yet it does mean
that 'Pity and Love' are not 'too venerable for the

imputation of Guilt'. So the Bard's song, which is 'According to the inspiration of the Poetic Genius', deals with fundamentals. The Bard 'took refuge in Milton's bosom', i.e. Milton accepted his song. Milton thereupon abandoned covenanted religion: 'He took off the robe of the promise & ungirded himself from the oath of God', and went naked (as on the title-page) 'to Eternal Death'. In the third full-page illustration he faces the spectator and holds the discarded robe in his left and the girdle in his right hand. A rising sun behind him is repeated in a rayed halo round his head.

Eternity is man's proper state or home. In it he is not bound down to five fixed senses. He has any number of senses which expand or contract at will.

> Why has not man a microscopic eye?
> For this plain reason, man is not a fly.

So Pope said, but in Eternity, Blake could have told him, man has a microscopic or any other eye at will. Nor is he subject to those two Kantian forms of perception, Space and Time. The mystic can transcend them, but the philosopher cannot. Milton descending saw Albion, i.e. Man, stretched dead 'upon the Rock of Ages . . . the Sea of Time & Space thunder'd aloud Against the rock'. Albion is described indifferently as asleep or dead. He is dead to Eternity instead of being alive to and in Eternity. Blake was so alive throughout his earthly existence and even had some fore-experience of the 'enlarged and numerous senses' which are essentially man's and which he regains in Eternity on being 'raised a spiritual body'. But now Milton is to go to Eternal Death, that is to the permanent death of his selfish centre, to the final and complete end of the self which was responsible for the errors of *Paradise Lost*. The result, of course, of passing through Eternal Death is Eternal Life, a life which by its very nature cannot, once found, end.

K

The journey of Milton 'unhappy tho' in heaven' imitates, with important differences, that of Satan, who was unhappy in Hell, in *Paradise Lost*, a model already used for Urizen's journey in *The Four Zoas*, VI. Satan with evil intent journeyed from hell to the newly created terrestrial system where he found Adam: Milton with good intent journeyed, as the diagram in Book II shows, to the midst of the four 'Ruin'd Universes', Urthona, Urizen, Luvah, Tharmas, which intersect in the egg-shaped world containing both Satan and Adam. The 'Track that Satan first made' (*Paradise Lost*, X, Argument and 314) suggested 'Milton's Track' in the diagram, but, whereas Satan's journey is presented as an undertaking in space and time, Milton's journey was into space and time. In *Paradise Lost* Hell, Chaos and the World have a physical existence, in *Milton* Blake describes a spiritual journey and spiritual events by means of his predominantly pictorial imagination: he is difficult because the processes of the seen world are so very different from those of the unseen.

In September 1802 Wordsworth invoked Milton:

Milton! thou shouldst be living at this hour.

Blake knew that Milton was still alive and that that great poet, whose magnificent visions he loved to depict, could not fail to reject the errors of his mortal years. Wordsworth would have liked him to be revegetated on earth, for Blake that would be useless. He must come back to a spirit still here, just as Robert did—or rather Robert had never lost contact. For Milton to make contact with the still vegetated William was the same as making contact with the released Robert: so in the fourth and fifth full-page pictures respectively Milton as a star enters William's left and Robert's right foot. Milton living at this hour might well mean a terrifying intensification of 'Milton's Religion' with all its evils, but Los in Blake is confident.

I recollect an old Prophecy in Eden, recorded in gold, and oft
Sung to the harp, That Milton, of the land of Albion,
Should up ascend forward from Felpham's Vale & break the Chain
Of Jealousy from all its roots.

Even so had Satan known 'of a new World and new kind of Creature to be created, according to an ancient Prophesie or report in Heaven' (*Paradise Lost*, I, Argument, and II, 346).

This descent of Milton was not a poetic fancy or a trick of mythological machinery. Blake had another of his great inner experiences which he interpreted in this way after it had happened.

But Milton entering my Foot, I saw in the nether
Regions of the Imagination . . .
. . . the vast breach of Milton's descent.
But I knew not that it was Milton, for man cannot know
What passes in his members till periods of Space & Time
Reveal the secrets of Eternity: for more extensive
Than any other earthly things are Man's earthly lineaments.
And all this Vegetable World appear'd on my left Foot
As a bright sandal form'd immortal of precious stones & gold.
I stoopèd down & bound it on to walk forward thro' Eternity.
. . . what time I bound my sandals
On to walk forward thro' Eternity, Los descended to me;
And Los behind me stood, a terrible flaming Sun, just close
Behind my back. I turnèd round in terror, and behold,
Los stood in that fierce glowing fire; & he also stoop'd down
And bound my sandals on in Udan-Adan . . .
And I became One Man with him arising in my strength.

It was at Felpham that Blake came to full consciousness of the 'immortal' beauty of the physical world. He connects this with Milton's descent and it led straight to Blake's identification with Los. Now, as not before, he felt in himself the full force of the poetic-prophetic genius working in Time: Los steps from the Sun, in the fourth full-page picture, and Blake, who is binding on his sandals (note the plural, the right or spiritual foot is also shod), turns 'round in terror'. It was a moment comparable to the touching of Isaiah's lips with a live coal from off the altar or to Ezekiel's vision of the fire infolding itself.

This was illumination: it was also a stage in integration. 'Resurrection to Unity' was always Blake's objective from *All Religions Are One* and *The Marriage of Heaven and Hell* to the complete integration of the final pages of *Jerusalem*. He could not rest in any sort of dualism. A mere Urizen-Orc antithesis led nowhere. A dualism of soul and body or of spirit and matter was no better. 'Man has no Body distinct from his Soul', said 'The voice of the Devil' in *The Marriage of Heaven and Hell*, making a very different approach from the 'plain man' of to-day who says man has no soul distinct from his body. So now, united with Los who works in Time, Blake sees the 'immortal' beauty of the physical world. The quite wonderful passage from—

Thou seest the Constellations in the deep & wondrous
    Night

to—

These are the Sons of Los, These the Visions of Eternity
        (25^{66}–26^{10}; 27-8 Keynes)

goes on—

But we see only as it were the hem of their garments
When with our vegetable eyes we view these wondrous
    Visions.

Here in the imaginative vision of nature, through not with the eye, Blake and Wordsworth were at one. Peter Bell suffered from 'Single vision and Newton's sleep'.

The pilgrim to and 'thro' Eternity' has shod his left foot with the 'Vegetable World'. This is a positive result of Milton's descent. Milton, having descended, is engaged almost throughout the poem in a struggle with Urizen like and unlike that of Jacob near Mahanaim.

. . . with cold hand Urizen stoop'd down
And took up water from the river Jordan, pouring on
To Milton's brain the icy fluid from his broad cold palm.
But Milton took of the red clay of Succoth, moulding it with care
Between his palms and filling up the furrows of many years,
Beginning at the feet of Urizen; and on the bones
Creating new flesh on the Demon cold, and building him,
As with new clay, a Human form in the Valley of Beth Peor.

The third full-page picture (reproduced in Binyon, the three-volume Nonesuch and Keynes, *William Blake's Engravings*) shows an advanced stage of this struggle. Urizen, who has his right leg in 'the streams of the brooks', has got beyond trying to freeze Milton's brain. With each hand he clutches a prohibitory Hebrew table of the law, but both Milton's hands are busily Humanizing him. On a hill above (almost a 'heaven') five players on musical instruments represent the Humanized (i.e. Divinized) senses, the imaginative vision of nature. Below the picture is a single line of text

To Annihilate the Selfhood of Deceit & False Forgiveness.

'Laws of . . . forgiveness' were proclaimed in *The Book of Urizen* (Chapter II) as if men could be made forgiving by act of parliament. Urizen is also the

author of social false forgiveness and of some forms of
the doctrine of the Atonement which Blake found
quite horrible.

To Humanize Urizen and to annihilate the Selfhood
are two aspects of the same activity. The Urizen of the
Lambeth books will be completely Humanized at the
end of *Jerusalem*. In *The Book of Urizen* the Fall
began with Urizen's separation of himself into a Selfhood. Thence came 'Milton's Religion' of God as a
punisher, that is Druidism with its stony temples and
human sacrifices. The rejection of Milton's errors can
only come about by the annihilation of the Selfhood.
That has to go on constantly, and, therefore, in this
poem Milton can be in other places and doing other
things and yet be seen, quite near the end, still striving
'upon the Brooks': the processes of the unseen world
are different from those of the seen.

Milton has not only to annihilate his Selfhood, but
also to redeem his Emanation, though neither would
be possible without the other. The use of the singular
Emanation for the sum of a being's emanations or
affective feelings does not begin until after the original
version of *The Four Zoas*, in which emanations are
plural and unpersonified ('Lost! Lost! Lost! are
my Emanations!') and the word 'counterpart' is used
for the later personified Emanation: nor does the
method of the counterpart's creation, e.g. of Enitharmon from Los in *The Book of Urizen*, quite suggest
that of the later Emanation. Ideally, 'in Eternity', the
Emanation both proceeds from and remains integrally
one with the being from which it proceeds, as the Holy
Ghost proceeds from the Father and the Son. So in
Jerusalem 88[3]:

When in Eternity Man converses with Man they enter
Into each other's Bosom (which are Universes of delight)
In mutual interchange. And first their Emanations
    meet . . .

For Man cannot unite with Man but by their Emana-
tions,
Which stand both Male & Female[1] at the Gates of each
Humanity.

In the fallen world the disintegrated man and his
Spectre and his Emanation may form a trinity of
frustration. The Spectre struggles for a livelihood and
a career, the Emanation is imprisoned. One of the
poems Blake did not publish begins

> My Spectre around me night and day
> Like a wild beast guards my way;
> My Emanation far within
> Weeps incessantly for my sin.

Those whom a man loves embody what he loves.
The Emanation is, therefore, more than a mere
personification. Milton loved three wives and three
daughters: in them can be found what he loved. So
Milton here has a six-fold Emanation with a six-letter
name, Ololon. What Milton loved is 'scatter'd thro'
the deep' and so he must 'go into the deep, her to
redeem & himself perish'. What Milton loved loves
him and, dwelling in Eden or Eternity by 'a sweet
River of milk & liquid pearl', will both encourage
him in his decision to descend, will drive him 'Down
into Ulro' (this world below, which, it should be clearly
understood, was regarded by Blake not as an illusion
but as a delusion), and will then inevitably descend
also to save him. You can be in two places at once
when place is only metaphorical.

The decision of Ololon to descend is approved by
Jesus:

Watch over this World, and with your brooding wings
Renew it to Eternal Life. Lo! I am with you alway.
But you cannot renew Milton: he goes to Eternal Death.

[1] i.e. not divided into Male and Female

This is all part of the process which brings about the union of Blake with Los and the imaginative vision of the 'Vegetable World' in the latter part of Book I. In Book II we have the descent of Ololon and her meeting with Milton. Except in so far as a six-fold Emanation may not be wholly harmonious in itself (the three wives in the picture at the top of p. 16 look away from the three daughters), it is more helpful to think of Ololon not as the wives and daughters but as the sum of all Milton's affections as shown in his poems: it is there, even if he did have a faulty attitude to his womenfolk in his lifetime, that we should see what it is that both has to be redeemed and is itself a redeeming influence, as it certainly is: otherwise why should the nations see

the Lord coming
In the Clouds of Ololon with Power & Great Glory?

It is a Second Coming, so very different from, yet reminiscent of, the evil second coming of *Paradise Lost* x. There Sin and Death 'To make the way easier from Hell to this World to and fro ... pave a broad Highway or Bridge over Chaos': here 'a wide road was open to Eternity By Ololon's descent' and Ololon had followed Milton's track through the 'Chaoses' of the four 'Ruin'd Universes'. The parallel is deliberate and tells us where Milton had been wrong about his Emanation. He thought her Sin. He thought sexual passion sin. He thought the male should permanently dominate the female (Blake is all against the 'female will' but equally against the dominance of the masculine Spectre: in Eternity there is no division into male and female). Milton, the Puritan, believed in repression rather than integration. His Emanation was 'scatter'd thro' the deep' of his own mind. He had to redeem her, and the obverse of this process is the Humanizing or reintegration of Urizen and the annihilation of what is annihilable, the Selfhood.

The first stage of Ololon's descent is into Beulah, Bunyan's 'sweet and pleasant country . . . upon the borders of heaven'. It means 'married' (Isaiah lxii. 4). It is the earthly state next to Eden or Eternity. For those men who sometimes pass into Eden it is a rest from 'the great Wars of Eternity'. Others approach it from below and sometimes achieve its threefold vision which is short of the mystic's fourfold. It is the land of the arts, of Music and Poetry and Painting. The Daughters of Beulah are Blake's Muses. Beulah greets Ololon with a 'lamentation'. It is a lovely song of birds and flowers,[1] but it is followed by a rebuke to Ololon for the possessiveness of her love. The 'Divine Voice was heard . . . Saying':

When I first Married you, I gave you all my whole Soul;
I thought that you would love my loves & joy in my
    delights.

But it was not so, and this redemption of Ololon has another side to it.

        such your lot, to be continually Redeem'd
By death & misery of those you love & by Annihilation.

These high matters are first sung of in Beulah, 'where Contrarieties are equally True', where pity and fear are purged and even tragedy can bring repose, but Ololon must descend further, must make, accompanied by Daughters of Beulah who know their *Lycidas* and *Paradise Lost*—

[1] See p. 68.

. . . with soft melodious tears,
A long journey & dark thro' Chaos in the track of
    Milton's course,
To where the Contraries of Beulah War beneath
    Negation's Banner.

It is a world of disintegration, or, what is the same
thing,

. . . a dark land of death, of fiery corroding waters,
Where lie in evil death the Four Immortals pale and cold,
And the Eternal Man, even Albion, upon the Rock of
    Ages.
Seeing Milton's Shadow, some Daughters of Beulah
    trembling
Return'd; but Ololon remain'd before the Gates of the
    Dead.

And Ololon looked down into the Heavens[1] of Ulro in
    fear.
They said; 'How are the Wars of Man, which in Great
    Eternity
Appear around in the External Spheres of Visionary Life,
Here render'd Deadly within the Life & Interior Vision!
How are the Beasts & Birds & Fishes & Plants &
    Minerals
Here fix'd into a frozen bulk, subject to decay & death!
Those Visions of Human Life & Shadows of Wisdom &
    Knowledge
Are here frozen to unexpansive deadly destroying
    terrors;
And War & Hunting, the Two Fountains of the River of
    Life,
Are become Fountains of bitter Death & of corroding
    Hell,
Till Brotherhood is chang'd into a Curse & a Flattery
By Differences between Ideas, that Ideas themselves
    (which are
The Divine Members) may be slain in offerings for sin.

[1] See p. 38.

Here in a few lines, typical in style of the South Molton Street period, is the essence of Blake's prophecy —the contrast between Eternity or what man is meant to be and might be and the Rock of Ages of his narrow and deadly dreams. These lines are passionate, they are simple enough to one not wholly incorporated in the Rock, and, because they are poetry, they are sensuous. The sensuous images defeat the merely abstract reason and assist the imagination. Their character takes us back to the seventeenth-century Emblems and to the pictorialization of metaphor in such poems as George Herbert's *Love-Unknown*. The metaphysicals had been representatives of a considerable revolt against classicism, against 'the silly Greek & Latin slaves of the Sword', though their 'broken lights of thee' often seem at once tamer and more attainable than the tremendous visions of Blake, the Gothic poet born out of due time. Yet Blake can be Herbertian, as in *Jerusalem* 3: 'I pretend not to holiness; yet I pretend to love, to see, to converse with daily, as man with man, & the more to have an interest in the Friend of Sinners.'

Early in the morning, to the smell of wild thyme and the sound of the lark, to Blake, 'Walking in my Cottage Garden', Ololon appeared in the form of 'a Virgin of twelve years'. All the 'mighty Hosts' of which Ololon consisted, all that Milton had loved in heaven and earth, appeared in this 'Female Form' seeking Milton. It is not necessary to suppose that this exterior vision was of a flesh-and-blood child like Dante's first sight of Beatrice. At this 'spot of time', this crisis in the union of Blake-Milton-Los, Ololon was seen and spoke, in a mild voice but 'more distinct than any earthly'. It was 'as the Flash of lightning, but more quick' that she had stood in the garden, but a picture cannot show something moving quicker than light (i.e. as quick as thought): the illustration on this page consists of a sketch of Blake's cottage with himself walking in the garden and Ololon descending from the sky. She asked for Milton. Milton also descended into the garden 'clothèd in black: severe & silent he descended'. He has first to deal with Satan, who is his Spectre or the Urizenic Milton—and all this time the struggle of Milton and Urizen at the ford is going on. Satan is the sum of all false religions, all perversions of Christianity. That is what the hell of *Paradise Lost* symbolized.

I also stood in Satan's bosom & beheld its desolations,
A ruin'd Man, a ruin'd building of God not made with hands;
Its plains of burning sand, its mountains of marble terrible,
Its pits & declivities flowing with molten ore & fountains
Of pitch & nitre; its ruin'd palaces & cities & mighty works;
Its furnaces of affliction in which his Angels & Emanations
Labour with blacken'd visages among its stupendous ruins;
Arches & pyramids & porches, colonades & domes,
In which dwells Mystery, Babylon: here is her secret place:
From hence she comes forth on the Churches in delight:
Here is her Cup fill'd with its poisons in these horrid vales,
And here her scarlet Veil woven in pestilence & war.
Here is Jerusalem bound in chains in the Dens of Babylon.

Milton might be expected to destroy Satan or banish him for ever, to damn him as in *Paradise Lost*, but that was not the lesson of the Bard's Song. That would be using Satan to cast out Satan, an act of the priest who slew the slayer and shall himself be slain: to do that is to become what one beholds. To supersede one rationalist system by another, as Milton could easily do, is to remain in the net of rationalist system. To assert Self in a new and better way is still to assert Self. Milton comes

> . . . to Self Annihilation.
> Such are the Laws of Eternity, that each shall mutually Annihilate himself for others' good, as I for thee.

Satan is not impressed. He, like those others, declares he is God alone: he holds the Sword of Justice and will go on

> Till All Things become One Great Satan, in Holiness Oppos'd to Mercy, and the Divine Delusion, Jesus, be no more.

This is the challenge of the 'Reasoning Spectre' which must be reclaimed and burnt in the fires not of hell but of the purifying imagination. Redemption not Punishment. The work is a continuous one, as Ololon sees and tells Milton, who has now turned to her. Milton has settled the problem of his Spectre which must be reclaimed to the service of the whole man: it is part of himself, just as Los recognized the Spectre of Urthona 'as another Self' in *The Four Zoas* VII. Now comes the redemption of his Emanation. Ololon, as far as she is 'feminine' or 'sexual', represents false art and poetry, that which stops short at the phenomenal world and so destroys 'imagination By imitation of Nature's Images drawn from Remembrance'. True art is not μίμησις[1] as vulgarly understood. The purpose of art is to reveal 'the Human Lineaments' till 'Generation is swallow'd up in Regeneration'. The Virgin Ololon recognizes this and divides into Virgin and Ololon. The Virgin goes with Milton to Eternal Death. There is a final and complete end to that side of the Milton of *Paradise*

---

[1] Imitation.

Lost. That Milton believed in a rationalistic Universe governed by arbitrary laws, he accepted at face value the phenomenal world, he failed to make imaginative contact with Eternity. Great poet though he was, in him 'the Father is Destiny, the Son a Ratio of the five senses, & the Holy-ghost Vacuum', as Blake had said years ago in *The Marriage of Heaven and Hell*.

The reclamation of the Spectre and the redemption of the Emanation mean apocalypse. The continuous process of redemption by sacrifice of self, by the annihilation of all that is annihilable, means the appearance of Jesus 'clothèd in Clouds of blood, to enter Albion's Bosom, the bosom of death'. The four Zoas sound their trumpets of triumphal announcement.

Terror struck in the Vale I stood at that immortal sound.
My bones trembled, I fell outstretch'd upon the path
A moment, & my Soul return'd into its mortal state
To Resurrection & Judgment in the Vegetable Body;
And my sweet Shadow of Delight stood trembling by
    my side.

Catherine found William awakening from a swoon, and

Immediately the Lark mounted with a loud trill from
    Felpham's Vale.

Perhaps it was the same mounting lark that had met Ololon descending, for the whole of a great vision such as this can take place in a moment of the time measured by the sun or by the human pulse.

Every Time less than a pulsation of the artery
Is equal in its period & value to Six Thousand Years.
For in this Period the Poet's Work is Done; and all the
    Great
Events of Time start forth & are conciev'd in such a
    Period,
Within a Moment, a Pulsation of the Artery.
                        (*Milton*, 27⁶³–28³; 30–1, Keynes).

This moment of vision or inspiration is also depicted in the seventh full-page picture, where Albion and Jerusalem asleep on the Rock of Ages in the dark sea of Time and Space are visited by a clamorous eagle from the sunlit world of Eternity.

Jerusalem

In *Milton* Blake attacked on a narrow front, pressed all the time and reached his objective. In *Jerusalem* he attacks on a wide front and the battle is long and confused with many setbacks, but, when he wins it, he has won the war. *Jerusalem* is the longest of Blake's published poems. Its four 'chapters' are on a hundred plates and contain rather less than 5,000 lines including the prose parts of the four introductions. It is more than twice as long as *Milton* and is more richly illustrated. It is less easy to follow. The title-page, like that of *Milton*, is dated 1804, but no existing copy is on paper of an earlier date than 1818, and that is probably when its engraving was finished. Only nine complete engraved copies are known, of which three were made after Blake's death. There is only one fully coloured copy known, the one that belonged to Tatham.[1]

The first introduction is addressed 'To the Public', as the others are to the Jews, the Deists and the Christians respectively, but its most pregnant sentence, 'The Spirit of Jesus is continual forgiveness of Sin', might have been included in any one of the four. This introduction ends with a paragraph, in obvious imitation of Milton's note on 'The Verse' of *Paradise Lost*, in which Blake explains that his lines vary 'in cadence & number of syllables' according to their subject-matter. Then comes Chapter 1, 'Of the Sleep

[1] A reproduction of this copy in a limited edition for the William Blake Trust is expected as the present book goes through the press.

of Ulro and of the passage through Eternal Death and of the awaking to Eternal Life'. In fact Albion, in this chapter, remains asleep, but the first measures for his awakening are taken.

The heart of this chapter is to be found in the picture on p. 14[1] (reproduced in colours in Binyon, though wrongly described there). An examination of it will also show how very compact Blake's symbolism had now become. The picture, which occupies rather less than the lower half of the page, is enclosed in a half-circle rainbow the curve of which rests on the ground at each end. Full length on the ground lies Albion asleep, facing the spectator, his head supported by his left hand. Above him, upright in the air and a little reminiscent of the newly-created Eve, is his Emanation, Jerusalem, in a shield-shaped cloud. On her right are the waxing moon and four stars, on her left a single star.

Albion, personified England or Britain, now stands for Man, the symbolism of the part for the whole. Man is asleep and dreaming. Clear vision will only come when he wakes. (There is no suggestion, it may be noted, in Blake's work that he shared Wordsworth's peculiarity of having a more vivid visual imagination when dreaming than when awake—'The glory and the freshness of a dream'.) Here, as in *Milton*, Albion is dead to Eternity. He believes in the evidence of his senses and the survival of *qui peut*. Jerusalem, which is his soul's instinctive longing for and knowledge of Eternal Life, is a 'Phantom of the over heated brain' (4[21]). This disaster which has overtaken Albion, the Fall, may in one aspect be likened to the disaster which overtook the fabled island Atlantis when the ocean overwhelmed it. The Atlantic, therefore, regularly symbolizes the Sea of Error which has overwhelmed man: it has also, probably, a further bad sense in that

[1] See Plate IV.

And Los beheld the mild Emanation Jerusalem eastward, bending
Her revolutions toward the Starry Wheels in maternal anguish
Like a pale cloud arising from the arms of Beulahs Daughters:
In Entuthon Benythons deep Vales beneath Golgonooza.

JERUSALEM ABOVE THE SLEEPING ALBION
From JERUSALEM
Width of original design: 6·4″

it separates Europe from America, on which so many had cast longing eyes in the revolutionary years. Blake must have been fond of studying maps, and his habit of geographical symbolism is at its height in *Jerusalem*, where for the first time Erin appears. Erin or Ireland stretches north and south at right angles to the east-and-west Atlantic and acts as a breakwater for the 'Island White'. So, if there is anything which may keep from Albion the full force of an unchecked Atlantic of error, it may well be symbolized by Erin. Moreover, there is another symbol for protection from an all-destroying deluge, the rainbow which God set in the sky for that very purpose. Erin and the rainbow are, therefore, symbolically the same.

What, in fact, mitigates for Albion the rage of the Atlantic and constitutes a God-given promise for the future? Inspired art, Blake's own works. These works are given physical extension or material form: they are 'Spaces of Erin' (9^{34}, 11^{8-12}, 12^{22}): they are also 'Sons and Daughters of Jerusalem' (10^3) because she is their source, and 'Sons and Daughters of Los' (10^4 and 11^{11}) because it is Los's hard work at his shaping furnaces that gives them their form as 'Spaces of Erin'. So in this picture the rainbow is the inspired art, by means of which and under the protection of which Albion's Emanation may make an appearance though Albion still sleeps. The Starry Wheels, the wheeling heavenly bodies, move from east to west and Jerusalem goes out to meet them.

And Los beheld the mild Emanation Jerusalem eastward
    bending
Her revolutions toward the Starry Wheels in maternal
    anguish,
Like a pale cloud arising from the arms of Beulah's
    Daughters.

We know Blake's Muses.

L

The strenuous and struggling activity of the inspired artist is also symbolized as the building of the city of Golgonooza by Los. Before he can do that he must make the Spectre serve him. Pages 6 to 11 are mainly spiritual autobiography. The picture on p. 6 (reproduced in Wright, Bronowski, and Keynes, *William Blake's Engravings*) shows Los at his anvil arguing with the bat-winged Spectre above him. The familiar Felpham arguments reappear. The poet-prophet is threatened with poverty, is shown how he has fallen behind his contemporaries in worldly success, is told that his wrongheadedness has meant the repression of his affections. The twelve Sons of Albion, who, with his twelve Daughters, play a considerable part in *Jerusalem*, will get the better of him: these sons are the various types of ordinary fallen man. Los, however, is firm and makes the Spectre labour with him at the anvil. Blake was making himself a whole man, wasting nothing in mental discord. It meant the culmination of the process begun in *The Four Zoas*, VII, when Los accepted the Spectre of Urthona. So, 'terrified with admiration of Erin's spaces',

. . . they builded Golgonooza, terrible eternal labour.
(12^{24}).

From this city of inspired art may be obtained a vision of the real nature of the world and of the prophet's mission.

I see the Four-fold Man: the Humanity in deadly sleep,
And its fallen Emanation, the Spectre & its cruel Shadow.
I see the Past, Present & Future existing all at once
Before me. O Divine Spirit! sustain me on thy wings,
That I may awake Albion from his long & cold repose!
(15$^{6-10}$).

The false philosophies of Bacon, Newton, and Locke, for whom all knowledge comes from the five senses, have ruined 'the Schools & Universities of Europe' with their mechanistic rationalism. 'Cam is a little stream!' (5⁹). So we return to the vision of the fallen Albion, whose sons execrate Jerusalem, 'Mother of pity and dishonourable forgiveness'. Yet not only Jerusalem but also Vala, not only heavenly but also earthly love, lament Albion's state and its effect on themselves. They are as Mary and Martha. Jerusalem remembers the 'sweet regions . . . Where we delight in innocence before the face of the Lamb', but prudential Vala repents and blames. Jerusalem pleads for mutual forgiveness and reminds Vala that though she (Jerusalem) is the bride of the Lamb of God, Vala was given as bride to Albion. Having read *Milton* and learnt how to look at Nature, we know what this means.

Albion does not. Like Adam in Eden he is ashamed. He is covered with shame as Job was with boils. He is ashamed of Jerusalem and looks on Vala as sin. He cries out for punishment—after which he will hide in the very recesses of sin. Jerusalem in vain urges him to accept forgiveness rather than punishment 'with Iron Wheels of War'. Let Paris die in punishment for Helen: that is what Love and War have come to. The full-page picture at the end of this first chapter shows Jerusalem (who 'is named Liberty Among the Sons of Albion') looking in pitying horror at Hand, the eldest and representative of the Sons, who walks away from her in flames of torment, a serpent wound round his two outstretched arms, his head looking back at her in loathing—and perhaps in lingering but hopeless doubt.

In the introduction to the second chapter Blake finds a point of resemblance between Albion and the Adam Kadmon of the Jewish Cabbalah, and he calls on the Jews to return to 'Mental Sacrifice & War'. The poem in this introduction has already been discussed[1] in part, but lines 25, 6 recall *Jerusalem* 12²⁵⁻⁸:

---

[1] P. 133.

What are those golden builders doing? . . .
. . . Near Tyburn's fatal Tree? Is that
Mild Zion's hill's most ancient promontory, near mournful
Ever weeping Paddington? Is that Calvary and Golgotha
Becoming a building of pity and compassion?

The builders are the builders of Golgonooza. It was a wonderful thing to Blake that he should be building Golgonooza (New Golgotha) so near to Tyburn (Old Golgotha), which was only half a mile from South Molton Street. The corruption of religion had led to human sacrifices of every kind, including judicial execution. Of human sacrifice in general and judicial execution in particular the Crucifixion was the climax. Golgotha was Tyburn, and Tyburn was Golgotha. The last execution at Tyburn was on 7 November 1783, and Blake, as a boy and young man living only a mile away and very near to Oxford Street along which the processions passed from Newgate, must have been very familiar with Tyburn, but it is in the later poems that it is so often mentioned. The general forms of the single gallows and of the dolmen, which Blake drew so often, are not unlike. What the old triple gallows, which could hang three lots of eight at a time, looked like, Blake knew from Hogarth's picture of the 'Idle 'Prentice Executed at Tyburn': nor, caught up as he had been in the Gordon riots, would he forget what came after, 'when strings of boys under fourteen were hung up in a row to vindicate the offended majesty of the law. "*I never saw boys cry so!*" observed George Selwyn, connoisseur in hanging, in his *Diary*.'[1]

The building of Golgonooza to supersede Druid Tyburn is a continuous process: there is nothing static about Eternity. Urizen's original error in *The Book of Urizen* was to seek 'a solid without fluctuation'. Blake's

[1] Gilchrist.

heaven is no place of perpetual rest but one of mental
'War and Hunting', in which identities are preserved
but with such expansive powers that the claustro-
phobia of personal survival disappears. Blake believed
utterly in the 'Minute Particular', the individual soul.
Poet and Painter as he is of Liberty and Fraternity, he
never says a word in praise of Equality anywhere short
of Eternity (55⁷). The destruction of individuality,
the reduction of all to a smooth uniformity, is the last
horror. Watching the brickmakers at work, as he
watched the blacksmith or the weaver or the smoke
from the factory 'scatter'd . . . thro' non-entity' (5¹³),
Blake saw how they dashed the clay into the mould,
then turned the brick out of the mould on to a board
to be carried away to the drying-ground or the kiln.
As he watched, he thought of each brick as like a
human being turned into a degraded and standardized
soul, regimented as into a pyramid. The Israelites as
slaves in Egypt were such a regimented pyramid. They
had, as it were, gone back from Abraham to Abraham's
idolatrous father, Terah, or his ancestor, Heber. That
is the meaning of their oppression in Egypt: that is
what happens to modern regimented souls.

> . . . there they take up
> The articulations of a man's soul, and laughing throw it
>   down
> Into the frame, then knock it out upon the plank; &
>   souls are baked
> In bricks to build the pyramids of Heber & Terah.
>   (31⁹⁻¹²)

The compression of thought, speech, and imagery in
the last line could hardly be exceeded, but it is characteristic of *Jerusalem*.

The reference to Israel in Egypt is not accidental in
a chapter addressed to the Jews. The chapter deals
with the fallen world under Sinaitic Law and a religion

of 'sacrifice of (miscall'd) Enemies For Atonement',
as the hanging of seven sons of Saul to make 'atonement' (2 Samuel xxi. 3) to the Gibeonites or the hanging
by Joshua of the king of Ai and his subsequent erection
of an altar of unhewn stones (Joshua viii. 29–31 and
Jerusalem 28²¹, ²). Sacrifice implies a sense of guilt
and of a need for punishment: at the same time man
tries to choose his own form of punishment and to
retain the sin as we have seen in the first 'chapter'.
This is the Old Testament, and present day, 'Man of
Sin & Repentance' (29¹²), whose religion may be called
Rahab after the harlot who saved her own skin by helping the Israelites to take Jericho, a false spiritual
religion (a 'System of Moral Virtue', 39¹⁰, which
Blake *would* call Rahab) intimately allied with the false
naturalistic religion called Tirzah. It leads him to
idolatrous worship of a God who is only 'his own
Shadow' (29⁴⁶) and to address to it 'words of eternity'
which ought to be addressed to the Divine Vision. He
forgets the unity of spirit, that in Eternity Man is
Divine and God is Human, which is what is meant by
the Divine Humanity of Jesus. Blake was entering
fully into the meaning of his own words *To Tirzah*:

> The Death of Jesus set me free:
> Then what have I to do with thee?

From the ruin of Man and the loss of his eternal
powers something is always saved, Los's Spectre and
his Emanation. At such times as they are reintegrated
into Los there is someone to understand what is
happening and to struggle to rebuild Jerusalem, though
all that he, like Jeremiah, sees left is 'the ruins of the
Temple' (31⁴¹) and though the Sons of Albion defy
him continuously. So, perhaps because of the survival
of Los, there is one heartening mercy. Limits have
been set to the Fall. Withered as he is from Eternity,

Man has reached his worst: 'the limit of Contraction is named Adam' (42^{31}), i.e. Adam marks the point beyond which contraction goes no further and he is the particular limit which consists of contraction ('of' is both objective and descriptive), and, similarly, the Satan in him is 'the limit of Opakeness'—he won't get stupider than that.

Los has not everything to do himself. He has on his side the Saviour—

Displaying the Eternal Vision, the Divine Similitude,
In loves and tears of brothers, sisters, sons, fathers and
    friends,
Which if Man ceases to behold, he ceases to exist.

(38^{11-13}).

The Saviour goes on to explain the nature of life in Eternity where all are members of Christ and where, though there may be trespass, there is no sin because of forgiveness.

       . . . and he in us and we in him
Live in perfect harmony in Eden, the land of life,
Giving, recieving, and forgiving each other's trespass.
He is the Good shepherd, he is the Lord and master;
He is the Shepherd of Albion, he is all in all.

The ding-dong struggle goes on, and every page but one in this second chapter is illustrated and many of the illustrations are among Blake's most striking. The eleven lines of p. 37 are set between an upper picture of the Saviour supporting Albion as he collapses by the tree of vegetable life and a lower one of Albion stretched out on his couch of death with his bat-winged Spectre above him. On p. 46 (reproduced in Binyon and the Oxford edition) is the picture of a chariot of fire not taking Elijah to heaven nor fulfilling the purpose for which Blake summoned it in *Milton* ('Bring me my Chariot of fire !') but drawn sluggishly by two human-headed bulls of passion harnessed with serpents of materialism or, at best, mere Orc-like revolution. The serpents also form the wheels of the chariot. On the backs of the bulls are small eagle-headed figures ('When thou seest an Eagle, thou seest a portion of Genius', *The Marriage of Heaven and Hell* 9) who provide the only vivacity in the picture: one is giving a pen to a hand emerging from the curled horn of one of the bulls. In the chariot[1] sits a bearded Albion with downcast but not closed eyes, and by his side his Emanation sleeps. In this second chapter the way to redemption has been shown but redemption is still far off. Sin presses heavily on man. The chapter ends

Come then, O Lamb of God, and take away the remembrance of Sin.

After that comes (p. 51) a full-page picture (reproduced in Figgis, the three-volume Nonesuch, and the 1906–28 Gilchrist) of Vala crowned and bowed and, beside her, two of the Sons of Albion, Hyle and Skofeld, in utter misery.

The third chapter, with an introduction 'To the Deists', marks an advance in historical time. Deism, 'belief in the existence of God not as a revealed certainty but as a hypothesis required by reason',[2] otherwise 'Natural Religion' which Blake had combated from the first, must, from its wrong approach, its denial of spiritual primacy, be itself wrong. In the eighteenth century it had not only taken an anti-Christian form: it had also permeated official Christianity and Christian apologetics. Wesley and

---

[1] This chariot should have a bearing on the interpretation of the chariot, or possibly chariots, in the recently discovered picture by Blake (now in the Tate Gallery) which Mr. Keynes described in *Country Life* for 11 November 1949.

[2] *Pocket Oxford Dictionary.*

Whitefield had represented real Christianity, 'enthusiasm' in its proper sense. Deism meant fatal generalities such as that of the 'Friend of Humanity' satirized in *The Anti-Jacobin*, it meant 'Vengeance for Sin' instead of forgiveness, it meant war-mongering. 'All the Destruction, therefore, in Christian Europe has arisen from Deism, which is Natural Religion.' It is a continuation of Rahab. It is Druidism. Its greatest triumph was the Crucifixion, but the Crucifixion was, and is, voluntarily suffered by the Saviour, who knows that Satan cannot be overcome by Satanic means but by forgiveness and that a man must die to save not only his friend but his enemy. The Crucifixion, then, in this double aspect, is the central subject of Chapter III, and the first and last pictures represent, respectively, Deism and Christ.

The first picture is reproduced by Binyon, who, following Foster Damon, wrongly describes it as representing Beulah. That is impossible, if only because Beulah is never personified. Wright gets nearer with Vala. It shows a richly clothed female figure, her smooth face cupped in both hands, her eyes closed, on a sort of winged throne of which the wings contain earth, moon, and stars. She and her throne are on an outspread sunflower, thus preventing its seeds from aspiring (see *Songs of Experience*). On her head is a triple crown, and above that can be seen, at least in the coloured copy, what may be a royal crown or a helmet. It is not essential to give her a name: the pictorial vision cannot always be translated exactly into the verbal inspiration. She is primarily a 'female will', beautiful and sinister. Helmet or no helmet, she is 'Religion hid in War' (75^{20}): so we will call her Rahab.

The last picture (reproduced in Binyon, the three-volume Nonesuch and the 1906–28 Gilchrist) has already been described[1] from the point of view of composition,

[1] p. 36.

and the fact that Albion is the youth of 'Glad Day' has
been pointed out. In that lies the explanation of what
has caused a good deal of confusion in the interpretation
of Blake. Blake is all of a piece, say some, and they try
to construct a system of Blakean doctrine on texts
drawn from any of his writings, early or late, published
or unpublished. Blake developed and changed, say
others, and then they find themselves confronted with
the identity of early and late pronouncements. It was,
in fact, the same Blake throughout who held to the
primacy of the spiritual world and took that as his way
of life, but as he lived he learnt: he rejected error and
embraced newly-learnt truth: he had his great moments
of revelation. What sort of prophet would he have
been if he had never learnt anything fresh? He continued to produce copies of his older pictures and
poems, and he probably felt the same about his own
work as about the Bible: it is all fundamentally true,
but that does not prevent it from containing a pro-
gressive revelation. In particular Blake came to lay
more and more emphasis on forgiveness. In this
chapter, in which the physical birth of Jesus precedes
his crucifixion, forgiveness is exemplified by Joseph
who forgave Mary who was with child but not by him.
You cannot have forgiveness unless there has been a
fault. *O felix culpa* is an old cry. Joseph's anger is
turned away by Mary's love: he is no Theotormon.
The whole passage is of great beauty.

... 'If you Forgive one-another, so shall Jehovah Forgive
    You;
That He Himself may Dwell among you.' Fear not then
    to take
To thee Mary thy Wife, for she is with Child by the
    Holy Ghost.

Mary becomes identified with Jerusalem, the Emanation. Just as Mary had at first been rejected by Joseph

so had Jerusalem, in the words of Ezekiel (xvi. 5), been cast out to the loathing of her person. Now Mary and Jerusalem can sing a *Magnificat*.

Yet 'Times passèd on. Jerusalem fainted over the Cross & Sepulcher', and once more in the age of Deism 'A Harlot I am call'd'. This Magdalen, however, beholds the 'Spiritual Risen Body', and Jesus remains 'the Resurrection & the Life'. 'Los beheld the Divine Vision. . . . Therefore he livèd and breathèd in hope.' In hope, but the crucifixion goes on. Strong and active in Deism are those forces which crucified Jesus, which burnt the Druid victims in those monstrous wicker-cages, which appeared in the religion of Thor and Friga and which offered Rosamond the choice of knife or poison-cup. They are responsible for the horror of factory life in the early nineteenth century, for the press gang and the battlefield. Back they take us to Stonehenge (how like Wordsworth's vision on Salisbury Plain in 1793 when the Reign of Terror was going on in Paris and war had begun between France and England). Men and women actually enjoy the agony they inflict (65⁵⁸), 'rejoicing in Giant dance' (said[1] to be the Celtic name for Stonehenge). No different in principle were the human sacrifices of the Mexicans, where the victim's breast was opened with a flint-knife, his heart torn out, his skin stripped and worn by the priest and his body eaten by his captor (66-8). Nowadays it is the Daughters of Albion who so sacrifice humanity: for, whereas Blake conceives unimaginative reason as masculine, he conceives unimaginative cruelty and desire for domination as feminine. This 'female will' is Rahab, 'Religion hid in War', and her ally is Tirzah who restricts us for our good.

---

[1] Palgrave, *History of the Anglo-Saxons.*

'O thou poor Human Form!' said she. 'O thou poor
  child of woe!
Why wilt thou wander away from Tirzah? why me
  compel to bind thee?'

So, in the picture in *Songs of Experience*,[1] the boy
must have his hair combed.

It goes on. From Adam to Luther Blake reckoned
there had been twenty-seven Churches, erring in their
different ways. 'As the Church of *Jerusalem*, *Alex-
andria*, and *Antioch* have erred; so also the Church of
Rome hath erred', says the nineteenth Article of
Religion: add the Church of England and Blake would
subscribe. The erring churches go round 'in Eternal
Circle' and 'where Luther ends Adam begins again'.
Yet there is hope in any movement. Better the
'Starry Wheels' than an unmoving heaven. And the
next page contains the picture of Albion and Jesus.

The introduction to the fourth chapter is addressed
'To the Christians'. After a preliminary quatrain
('I give you the end of a golden string') comes wholly
enthusiastic prose. 'I know of no other Christianity
and of no other Gospel than the liberty both of body
& mind to exercise the Divine Arts of Imagination—
Imagination, the real & eternal World of which this
Vegetable Universe is but a faint shadow, & in which
we shall live in our Eternal or Imaginative Bodies,
when these Vegetable Mortal Bodies are no more. The
Apostles knew of no other Gospel. . . . Let every
Christian, as much as in him lies, engage himself
openly & publicly before all the World in some Mental
pursuit for the Building up of Jerusalem.' In the
succeeding blank verse poem Lear's 'Wheel of fire' is
identified with the Wheel of Natural Religion which,
striving against the real current of creation, confines
man to the mere phenomenal. It is Caiaphas against

[1] See p. 59 and Plate II.

Jesus, a contrast fully developed in the unpublished *Everlasting Gospel* of which the often unpolished couplets may have been written in the Rossetti MS. at much the same time as the first impressions of *Jerusalem* were being taken. The introduction ends with the last of Blake's pure lyrics, a call on England to awake and—

> Recieve the Lamb of God to dwell
>   In England's green & pleasant bowers.

That will come later. There is a good deal to go through before we come to the happy ending. Until then Jerusalem is in that condition of ruin, captivity and abandonment described by Jeremiah in *Lamentations*. Once it was far different. When England was the spiritual Israel, it was a blessing to the whole Earth.

> London cover'd the whole Earth, England encompass'd
>   the Nations,
> And all the Nations of the Earth were seen in the Cities
>   of Albion.

Jerusalem laments. We must remind ourselves that all this really goes on in the minds of men, in our own minds. The poet only makes it articulate. Alongside our deep-seated mourning for lost spirituality, which once existed, if not historically, at least ideally, there is another sorrow—'Beside her Vala howl'd upon the winds in pride of beauty'. The love of 'Nature', isolated from spirituality, means continual regret together with a fear that, if Jerusalem returned, this cherished and specifically feminine love would be lost.

> O rent in sunder from Jerusalem the Harlot
>   daughter
> In an eternal condemnation, in fierce burning flames
> Of torment unendurable! And if once a Delusion be found
> Woman must perish & the Heavens of Heavens remain
>   no more.

$$(80^{12\text{-}15})$$

It is precisely Francis Thompson in *The Hound of Heaven*—

> For, though I knew his love Who folloẁed,
> Yet was I sore adread
> Lest, having Him, I must have naught beside.

Vala wants to be pardoned and retain the offence.

> Pity me then, O Lamb of God ! O Jesus, pity me !
> Come into Luvah's Tents and seek not to revive the Dead.

The Dead is Albion. The jealous 'female will' would have Christianity to possess it, not to surrender to it. This is very nearly the last enemy to be destroyed. It is no Natural Religion based on a rationalist theory which denies intuitive knowledge, but one based on love of beauty and by no means wholly unspiritual. Yet it can only lead to the substitution of a dragon of war and materialism for the crucified:

> To weave Jerusalem a body according to her [Vala's] will,
> A Dragon form on Zion Hill's most ancient promontory.

Bringing in Christianity as an accessory to Nature worship results also in the worship of woman, the excesses of chivalric or romantic love, and a female dominance as successful and deleterious as that of the wife of Bath though generally achieved by less direct methods. We have already met this in *Europe*, where lovely Woman has dominion in the night of Enitharmon's joy, and the Warriors of *Jerusalem* 68 know woman as the instigator of war—

> I must rush again to War; for the Virgin has frown'd & refus'd.

This is the point and context of the doings of the two daughters of Albion, Cambel and Gwendolen. They are the counterparts of the two leading sons of Albion, Hand and Hyle, whom they subdue respectively to their will. Blake may be interpreting the lives of persons actually known to him, but it is the interpretation and its universal application that matter. The setting on Skiddaw and the Derbyshire hills only means that Blake found them on his map as barren masses suitable for unspiritual acts, just as Albion sleeps on his Rock of Ages. Gwendolen reduces Hyle to a state of childish dependence on her and then finds he has sunk into the merely material: the 'infant Love' has become 'a winding Worm', but Gwendolen is 'perfect in beauty' (82⁴⁹). Cambel, trembling with jealousy, succeeds in turning even mighty Hand also into an infant, though she has to bind 'his wrists & ankles with the iron arms of love'.

One of the means of success is subtle lying: Gwendolen instructs the whole sisterhood. The picture on p. 81 makes it all much clearer. There Gwendolen is portrayed with her back to the spectator, holding the falsehood (82¹⁷) in her *left* hand behind her back, having her left foot crossed in front of the right, and with her right hand pointing to a quatrain which extols forgiveness as heavenly but non-forgiveness as more profitable on earth—'especially to the Female'. Facing the spectator is Cambel in a conventional Venus pose. The ten other daughters of Albion hang on Gwendolen's words. Gwendolen's falsehood is double. She claims the highest authority for it ('I heard Enitharmon say to Los') and it is identical with Vala's false aim of making the best of both worlds. They will live in Babylon and create their own Jerusalem. Man will exhaust his energies in war, and 'Woman permanent remain' (82³⁵). We have come back by this different route to Rahab, 'Religion hid in War'. We were led to it before by the perverted masculine will, now by the perverted female will. In Eternity there is no marrying or giving in marriage, no division into sexes.

Nevertheless, Los, who was once set to watch Urizen and keep him apart from Eternity, now with his attentive Spectre (83 78) watches that Albion may be reunited with Eternity. If England is not awake, Blake is. There are signs that spirituality survives. The daughters of Albion self-exiled to the waters of Babylon long for Jerusalem. Los sings a song in praise of Jerusalem (p. 85) and from this point on there is no stopping him. He brushes aside the last effort of his own Emanation to retain a feminine separateness: in fact both Spectre and Emanation, while mostly working harmoniously with Los, will continue, in this world, to be occasionally centrifugal and selfish. They work in with Los so well that he at last has a complete vision of Antichrist, 'the Covering Cherub', a name taken from Ezekiel and denoting both the Cherub whose flaming sword kept Adam from Eden and the Cherub which covered and hid the Mercy Seat. It is a complete vision of the fundamental evils with which we have battled throughout *Jerusalem*. It supplies what was missing in the apocalypse of *The Four Zoas*. There Orc's inadequacy had not yet been found out: Revolution might still save the world. A conviction that he was on the wrong lines was probably one reason why Blake never published that poem. Now Blake had learnt that to give error a body or form enables it to be rejected. This is the Last Judgement. 'Sheep . . . Goats' he wrote at the head of the introduction to the first chapter of Jerusalem. Separate the goats and you have the sheep. See Antichrist as Antichrist and you see Christ as Christ.

Nothing now 'can withstand the fury of my course among the stars'. No rearguard action by Natural Religion avails at all. No religion that is not wholly spiritual has any value. Sacraments are worse than useless if God is not recognized as 'the intellectual fountain of Humanity'. Los's integration is completed. England awakes on Albion's bosom. Albion awakes.

Then Jesus appearèd standing by Albion, as the Good Shepherd
By the lost Sheep that he hath found: & Albion knew that it
Was the Lord, the Universal Humanity; & Albion saw his Form
A Man, & they conversèd as Man with Man, in Ages of Eternity.
And the Divine Appearance was the likeness & similitude of Los.

This was much better than Sinai where 'the Lord spake unto Moses face to face, as a man speaketh unto his friend'.[1] Sinai led to the crucifixion from the point of view of the crucifier: this leads to it from the point of view of the crucified.

As at the Transfiguration a cloud overshadows them. It is 'the Covering Cherub coming on in darkness' and it divides Jesus and Albion. Albion is terrified 'not for himself but for his Friend Divine'. Ready to sacrifice himself to save Jesus he 'threw himself into the Furnaces of affliction': at once all was 'a Dream: the Furnaces became Fountains of Living Waters flowing from the Humanity Divine'. He calls on Jerusalem to awake. Everything is integrated: everything takes its proper place. As in *Milton*, what is annihilable is annihilated ('The Druid Spectre was Annihilate'), but Bacon, Newton, and Locke appear among the chariots of the Almighty. Man is in Eternity living the life of Imagination. And everything is Human.

[1] Exodus xxxiii. 11.

M

And I heard the Name of their Emanation: they are
   namèd Jerusalem.

After that Blake was so uplifted that he wrote not
'Finis', as at the end of *Milton*, but 'The End of The
Song of Jerusalem'.

The apparent amorphousness of *Jerusalem* begins to
disappear as we grow in understanding of it. Its
'spiritual form' is unlike that of any other poem and
therefore takes some finding out. Blake's thought
moves very fast, a great deal can happen in a few lines,
and the unpractised reader is liable to think that Blake
has wandered when it is really the reader who has
failed to keep pace with him. Where much must still
be obscure to most, patience, learning, and imagination
are needed until the full meaning and the perfect form
emerge—above all imagination, and that cannot work
properly without the pictorial accompaniment. To
have the words only is often to have the Spectre without the Emanation.

Last Writings

The Everlasting Gospel (Blake's own name for one
section of this unfinished poem) was written, in 1818
or possibly a little later, in the last blank spaces of
Robert's notebook and elsewhere. Its object is to
proclaim that Jesus or Christ (he now uses the two
names indifferently) was concerned with Eternal Life
and Forgiveness, which is its condition and consequence, and not with the moral virtues. It is quite
easy to argue, especially from the point of view of
Caiaphas, that Jesus was not a good man. Even as a
child he ran away from his parents and was very
haughty about it. He was disrespectful and dis-
obedient to lawfully constituted authority. He en-
couraged immorality by stopping the punishment of

the woman taken in adultery. He kept bad company.
He lived parasitically on the labour of others. He might
even be called the murderer of his disciples, since he
was responsible for their having to be executed as
rebels against Church and State.

> And Caiaphas was in his own Mind
> A benefactor to Mankind.

Caiaphas, and other properly minded people, could not
possibly subscribe to the doctrine that Jesus was without sin. The moralistic Christian, who thinks of Jesus
as a humble, gentle, creature going about doing and
being good, would take the same view as Caiaphas if
he saw Jesus as I see him and as he really was.

> The Vision of Christ that thou dost see
> Is my Vision's greatest Enemy. . . .
> Thine is the friend of All Mankind,
> Mine speaks in parables to the Blind. . . .
> Both read the Bible day & night,
> But thou read'st black where I read white.

Some of the poem is lost, some of what we have
consists of alternative or revised versions of the same
part of the poem, none of it was published, and therefore none of it should be quoted as necessarily giving
expression in a final and satisfactory way to any of
Blake's ideas. Much of it is dramatic and must be
read with the speaker and context in mind.

It is not difficult to imagine why Blake left the poem
unrevised and unpublished. Some of it is too negative
and too argumentative to come as anything but an
anticlimax to the magnificent *finale* of *Jerusalem*. Why
go back to harry Newton as 'St. Isaac', when the
essential Newton has already been seen in a vision as
a chariot of the Almighty? Why not settle down to

speaking in parables to the blind instead of attempting the impossible miracle of opening the eyes of those who have no faith?

Instead of going on with *The Everlasting Gospel* he reissued *The Gates of Paradise*, the little book of emblems engraved and published in 1793. To it he prefixed ten lines in octosyllabic couplets and suffixed fifty more described as 'The Keys of the Gates' and two final decasyllabic quatrains addressed 'To the Accuser who is The God of This World'. He also added a few lines under some of the emblems. The whole was issued as *For the Sexes/The Gates of Paradise*. In it we have Blake's mature view of earthly life. The Gates of Paradise consist of Forgiveness. The opposite of that is Satan, the Accuser. Even Jehovah, when he had written the Ten Commandments on the tables of stone, hid them in the ark beneath his Mercy Seat. Yet it was those prohibitory and accusing commandments, not any lifegiving words from the New Testament, which frowned from the east wall in every church.

> O Christians, Christians! tell me Why
> You rear it on your Altars high.

Forgiveness is again the theme of Blake's last published poem *The Ghost of Abel*, which was occasioned by Byron's *Cain*. In the two plates of this last of Blake's relief-etchings the blood of Abel calls for vengeance. It had been said to Cain of Abel 'unto thee shall be his desire and thou shalt rule over him'. So, when Abel the victim is overcome by the murderous spirit of vengeance, he is indeed ruled by Cain. Satan the Accuser rises with crown and spear from the grave of Abel. Human sacrifice and judicial execution have begun: they will culminate in the Crucifixion. 'Thou shalt Thyself', says Satan to Jehovah, 'be Sacrificed to

Me, thy God, on Calvary.' Jehovah assents, for the Crucifixion, rightly understood, brings a fiery illumination which is a Last Judgement at which the Satan in any man chooses, like Milton, Eternal Death, the Self Annihilation of all that is annihilable. When that consummation has been achieved, Jerusalem has been built.

CHAPTER VI

CONCLUSION

WE do not ask about Blake, as we do about Wordsworth or Tennyson, why his best work was done before he was forty. He gives no countenance to any theory that the imagination is as mortal as the body. If he gave up poetry in his sixties, it was only because poetry was not his primary art. His painting and engraving went on with full industry and inspiration. Christianity and Art were indistinguishable. He was hard at work on the Dante series when he died.

Blake was little known as a poet in his lifetime for the obvious reason that his poetry was not published in the usual way. As a painter he influenced his young artist friends. A full generation after his death the Pre-Raphaelites recognized him as their precursor. Ruskin, moreover, could write that, in expressing conditions of glaring and flickering light, Blake was greater than Rembrandt. It was Gilchrist's *Life* (1863) which began to make Blake generally known. Before that a single publication in 1839 of *Songs of Innocence and Experience* was all that had been done since Blake's death to make his poetry accessible. After Gilchrist the *Songs* were again published (1866) as were *Poetical Sketches* (1868). In 1868 appeared Swinburne's *Essay*. In 1874 W. M. Rossetti published Blake's *Poetical Works*, though he gave himself wide powers as an editor. In 1893 E. J. Ellis and W. B. Yeats produced three volumes of text and interpretation, in which *The Four Zoas* was printed for the first time though very inaccurately. Between the Rossetti and the Ellis-Yeats editions quite a number of facsimiles were produced, and the Ellis-Yeats edition had the great merit of much facsimile reproduction, though not, of course, in colour. Real scholarship, resulting in a trustworthy text, came only in the twentieth century. John Sampson's bibliographical and textual work in the incomplete Oxford editions of 1905 and 1913 was followed by the Oxford edition of *The Prophetic Writings* edited by Professors Sloss and Wallis (1926). In 1921 Geoffrey Keynes had produced his monumental bibliography and in 1925 his magnificent three-volume complete edition for the Nonesuch Press: in 1927 there followed the Nonesuch complete one-volume edition. Thus one hundred years after Blake's death all that survives of his writings, published or not, was for the first time generally available. There are a few words about which uncertainty can still be felt—Blake's doctrine of definite outline is not always exemplified in his handwriting—but for all practical purposes the text is firmly and finally established. That does not always apply to punctuation. There is very little punctuation in Blake's MSS. and much of that in the editions has been provided by the editors. Where a passage is difficult, punctuation may be guesswork, and mispunctuation may perpetuate misunderstanding. Therefore a reader who fails to understand a passage where the punctuation is not Blake's will sometimes be well advised to see what he can make of it without the punctuation which was meant to help him. One example must suffice. Blake wrote in the Rossetti MS. (p. 70):

The Last Judgment when all those are Cast away who trouble Religion with Questions concerning Good & Evil or Eating of the Tree of those Knowledges or Reasonings which hinder the Vision of God turning all into a Consuming fire

This is from *A Vision of the Last Judgment* and has no punctuation at all. All the editors put a comma after

'Vision of God': the next six words with 'turning' as a verbal adjective look grammatically innocuous but make no sort of sense, Blakean or ordinary. Remove the intruded comma and we at once see that 'turning' is a verbal noun and we have a tremendous and characteristically Blakean sense. These troublers prevent the Vision of God [from] turning everything into the consuming fire of the Last Judgement. For Blake the Vision of God constantly burns up the world (e.g. 'Then fell the Fires of Eternity', *The Four Zoas*, IX, 10).

Although in 1927 Blake was not, and still is not in the main, available in the stereoscopic form chosen by himself, the century-late provision of an adequate text gave his interpreters new opportunities. There have since that year been many notable works of interpretation and their number has been considerably increased since war ended in 1945. The present 'climate of opinion' may perhaps be more favourable to Blake than the Victorian, but the chief reason for belated study is belated material for study, for what was wanted was not what Blake might have read but what he had written. It is not necessary to be alarmed by finding that Blake obtained this or that bit of symbolism from the Jewish Cabbalah or the Hindu Scriptures or from astrology or from alchemy or from some other recondite source. It is the function of specialist students to provide help about these things, but they did not deeply influence Blake, though he used anything from any source which he felt could usefully illustrate his own thought. A good example is the Druidic symbolism so frequent in *Milton* and *Jerusalem*. Druidism came pat as a negation of Jerusalem: it gave no new direction to Blake's thought. What is necessary, because they affected both his thought and its expression, is as thorough a knowledge as possible of the Bible and Milton. Armed with those two, but not without them, the imaginative man may 'open his gates' to receive Blake.

If a distinction must be made between the poet and the picture-maker, it may well be that Blake will eventually be judged to stand higher in his primary art—the pictorial. His unique achievement is in the combination of the two and in his supremely spiritual quality. Wordsworth, of course, is at his best much superior to Blake in many ways, including mastery of verbal magic and music, but Blake lived habitually in a Promised Land from which Wordsworth withdrew into Egypt. For both of them the Mind of Man was 'My haunt, and the main region of my song'. For Wordsworth it is on Earth that 'We find our happiness, or not at all', nor had Blake any use for 'an allegorical abode where existence hath never come' (*Europe* 39). Wordsworth was thankful for 'obstinate questionings Of sense and outward things', but he was careful about letting himself go: 'Many times while going to school have I grasped at a wall or tree to recall myself from this abyss of idealism to the reality. . . . I was afraid of such processes.' Wordsworth called in one sense to redress the balance of another, but for Blake from *The Marriage of Heaven and Hell* onward the abyss is of the five senses and a tree represents the vegetative world by which Adam was deceived and on which Christ was crucified.

For Blake, with the probable exception[1] of a short period in middle life, was a Christian. He was even, as the only trained theologian to examine this question has shown, not so very far from being an orthodox Christian. He had the firmest belief in the real world of Eternity. He did not think that the phenomenal world is an illusion, but, if asked whether he believed in another world, he might well have made his point by saying

[1] Almost at the same time as Wordsworth: see Helen Darbishire, *The Poet Wordsworth* (1950), p. 137.

that his difficulty was to believe in this one. Although the Church 'Paul' figures among Blake's twenty-seven erroneous churches, he has much in common with St. Paul. It is true that Blake was an artist and that St. Paul had been brought up in a religion which, to keep its spirituality, classed the making of graven images with murder, theft and adultery, but for both the Law makes sin, for both Forgiveness is absolute and takes away all imputation of sin, Blake builds Golgonooza or Jerusalem, St. Paul's constant metaphor is building (edifying). Above all for both of them revelation was direct. Blake's direct contact with Eternity is matched by St. Paul's insistence that after Damascus he saw none of the apostles for three years and that the gospel he preaches 'is not after man. For I neither received it of man, neither was I taught it, but by the revelation of Jesus Christ' (Galatians i. 11, 12). Blake's vision in his cottage garden at Felpham was as absolute in its own way as St. Paul's on the road to Damascus, though it came at a later stage in his development. Both fell to the ground. Both kept the Divine Vision in time of trouble, both struggled throughout life not against flesh and blood but against spiritual evil in the 'heavens' of Man. St. Paul preached: for Blake 'Christianity is Art', the works demanded by his faith.

SELECT BIBLIOGRAPHY
(Twentieth Century)

I. EDITIONS OF BLAKE'S WRITINGS

1905 (reissued 1947). *The Poetical Works* (ed. Sampson). Oxford English Texts.

1913. *The Poetical Works* (ed. Sampson), textually enlarged. (Oxford Standard Authors edition.)

1925. *The Writings* (ed. Keynes), 3 vols. (Nonesuch.)

1926. *The Prophetic Writings* (ed. Sloss and Wallis), 2 vols.

1927 (reissued since). *Poetry and Prose* (ed. Keynes), the contents of the three-volume edition minus illustrations and notes and not in the strict chronological order of the three-volume edition.

1927. *Poems and Prophecies* (ed. Plowman, Everyman's Library).

1928. *Innocence and Experience* (ed. Wicksteed), with facsimile reproductions and full commentary.

II. PICTORIAL REPRODUCTIONS

1910 (revised and reissued, 1924). *Blake's Vision of the Book of Job*, by J. H. Wicksteed.

1912. *The Engravings of William Blake*, by A. G. B. Russell.

1922. *The Drawings and Engravings of William Blake*, by Laurence Binyon.

1925. *The Paintings of William Blake*, by Darrell Figgis (100 plates).

1926. *The Engraved Designs of William Blake*, by Laurence Binyon (82 plates).[1]

1935. *The Note-Book of William Blake called the Rossetti Manuscript*, by G. Keynes (complete facsimile with transcription).

1950. *William Blake's Engravings*, by G. Keynes.

[1] This, not the 1922 book, is referred to as 'Binyon' in the present volume.

III. BIOGRAPHY AND INTERPRETATION

1906. *Letters* and Tatham's *Life* (ed. A. G. B. Russell).

1906 (reissued, 1922 and 1928). Gilchrist's *Life* (ed. W. Graham Robertson).

1907. *William Blake*, by A. Symons (containing the early accounts of Blake except Tatham's.).

1921. *A Bibliography of William Blake*, by G. Keynes.

1924. *William Blake: His Philosophy and Symbols*, by S. Foster Damon.

1927. *An Introduction to the Study of Blake*, by Max Plowman.

1929. *The Life of William Blake*, by T. Wright (with many illustrations).

1929. *Blake and Modern Thought*, by D. Saurat.

1932 (revised and reissued, 1948). *The Life of William Blake*, by Mona Wilson.

1935. *Blake and Milton*, by D. Saurat.

1936. *William Blake*, by J. Middleton Murry.

1938. *William Blake's Circle of Destiny*, by M. O. Percival.

1940. *Windows of the Morning*, by M. R. Lowery.

1942 (revised and reissued, 1945). Gilchrist's *Life* (ed. Ruthven Todd, Everyman's Library).

1943. *A Man Without a Mask*, by J. Bronowski.

1946. *Blake: A Psychological Study*, by W. P. Witcutt.

1947. *Fearful Symmetry*, by N. Frye.

1948. *The Theology of William Blake*, by J. G. Davies.

1949. *English Blake*, by B. Blackstone.

1949. *Blake Studies*, by G. Keynes.

INDEX